EASY HIKING AROUND VANCOUVER

D0557398

Revised and expanded 7th edition
AN ALL-SEASON GUIDE

JEAN COUSINS

EASY HIKING

around

VANCOUVER

GREYSTONE BOOKS

Vancouver / Berkeley

Greystone Books Ltd.
www.greystonebooks.com

Cataloguing data available from Library and Archives Canada
ISBN 978-1-77100-024-6 (pbk.)
ISBN 978-1-77100-025-3 (ebook)

Editing by Lucy Kenward (seventh edition)
Copy editing by Shirarose Wilensky
Cover and text design by Jessica Sullivan
Cover photograph by Darryl Leniuk/Getty Images
Photographs by Ann Grant, Gillian Campbell, Vi Wall and Jean Cousins
Maps by Eric Leinberger from information supplied by the author
Printed and bound in Canada by Friesens
Distributed in the U.S. by Publishers Group West

We gratefully acknowledge the financial support of the Canada
Council for the Arts, the British Columbia Arts Council, the
Province of British Columbia through the Book Publishing Tax
Credit and the Government of Canada through the Canada Book
Fund for our publishing activities.

Greystone Books is committed to reducing the consumption of
old-growth forests in the books it publishes. This book is one step
toward that goal.

CONTENTS

Hiking routes change: brush grows up, trees fall, creeks flood and sweep away bridges, roads and buildings encroach on open spaces. Once again we have tramped the trails to ensure that *Easy Hiking around Vancouver* remains a reliable guide. This time around we have revised many hikes to reflect trail changes and have removed others that no longer seem suitable for novice and casual hikers. We have introduced nineteen new trips, including wilderness hikes and local winter walks, and have added notes on nearby campgrounds and sections accessible by wheelchair. We have also suggested how you might reach some starting points by public transit.

Updating a guidebook is work for many hands—and feet. I thank Ann Grant, Barbara Loewi, Gillian Campbell, Ann Gillmore and Eva Worm for their loyal support. They were more than hiking companions: they ferreted out facts and took photographs; they kept the project alive with their ideas and enthusiasm. We had fun.

I am grateful also for the help and material provided by the staff of provincial, regional and city parks, the B.C. Forest Service and the willingness of the hiking fraternity to share information and experience. I acknowledge, too, the expertise of the editorial staff at Greystone Books in putting the material together and thank Senior Editor Lucy Kenward for her contributions and guidance.

Finally, though not least in importance, I recognize the work of the various hiking groups, organizations and individuals who create, maintain and fight for our precious wilderness trails. Without their dedication, we could not go forth, book in hand, for a great day's hiking.

> INTRODUCTION

This guidebook is intended for anyone who is interested in hiking in the Vancouver area. It is designed to show the beginner how to set about hiking and where to go. In particular, it is an invitation to the non-expert to venture along wilderness trails. The novice or out-of-practice hiker can find his or her own level among the hikes suggested. Those with children can choose a short, designated family hike, on which there are likely to be picnic facilities or things of historical or natural interest. Elderly walkers can explore many of the trails suggested; alternative suggestions are often given for those who do not want to go all the way. The midweek hiker can use the book as a guide when club outings are not available, and the more advanced hikes can be enjoyed by enthusiasts according to their level of energy and fitness. For visitors to Vancouver, the hikes may be an introduction to the various wilderness areas within reach of the city.

Most of the hikes described are within one hour's driving time of Vancouver; many are close to the city and can be reached by public transit. A few are farther afield and may entail staying a night in a nearby town or campsite. All the hikes follow established routes. The hikes are graded according to the degree of difficulty, but all come within the ability of the non-expert.

Notes on recommended equipment, survival, walking techniques and natural history are included as an aid to the enjoyment of hiking.

Doctors and physical fitness experts tell us to walk more to stimulate our hearts and loosen up our joints, but there is also psychological healing that comes with walking. Striding out into the wilderness satisfies the spirit of adventure so rarely appeased by urban life and provides an antidote to stress. Moreover, walking is fun.

However out of practice you are today, this book will encourage you to begin walking—and to walk regularly for the rest of your life.

A short hike on well-kept trails requires very little special equipment: Comfortable walking shoes, sensible clothes and some weather protection are all you need. Those intending to venture on wilderness trails will enjoy choosing from the excellent and sophisticated hiking gear available in outdoor stores. We offer the following suggestions:

BOOTS ARE BEST
Wilderness trails, even when maintained faithfully, are rugged by nature. You need boots to support your ankles, and to cushion your feet and keep them dry—boots that will give you a grip on rock, snow, mud and scree.

While the less expensive trail shoes might be adequate for the occasional hiker, proper hiking boots are best. Go to a reputable outdoor store and ask for lightweight day-hiking boots with Vibram soles. When you buy your boots, wear the socks you will be hiking in. Allow room for your toes to spread, but be sure the boots fit snugly at the heel and are not so short that your toes push against the front of the boot at every downhill step. Wear the new boots on a few short walks before tackling an all-day hike in them.

You will come to love your boots as old friends. No other piece of equipment is more important to your hiking enjoyment. Take care of them: Wipe them off after use and dry them gently away from direct heat, then treat them with a good waterproofing compound or wax, and they will be ready for your next hike.

ABOUT SOCKS
Look for merino light-hiker socks in your local outdoor store. Some hikers like to wear lightweight polypropylene liners beneath heavier wool socks. If you favour this arrangement, you might try the double-layer socks now available.

DRESS IN LAYERS

Layered clothing is the key to comfort out of doors. You will be coping all day with changing conditions—weather, terrain and your own physical stamina. At first you may be chilly, then after 10 minutes you may be perspiring. The sun comes out and goes in again. The breeze that felt wonderful on your face as you were climbing seems to go right to your bones when you stop to rest. The idea is to keep your body temperature even, which is easier to do if you wear layers of lightweight clothes that you can peel off and put on as needed.

Your inner layer, i.e., underwear, should be a quick-drying synthetic. Next, wear a wool or cotton-blend shirt with synthetic or wool-blend pants. Coupled with a fleece vest, this arrangement will see you through much of the year. Jeans are not warm enough for winter and are horribly binding and heavy when wet. In summer, loose-fitting, lightweight pants are a good choice or pants that convert into shorts. In addition, you should carry a long-sleeved, all-wool sweater. For the hiker, there is no substitute for wool, which is light and moisture resistant, breathes and provides warmth even when wet. Your outer layer is a jacket made of waterproof, breathable fabric, such as Gore-Tex.

Rain gear is a matter of preference. Nylon-coated rain suits that go over your clothes will keep you dry in a deluge, if you don't mind the restriction. A poncho is better and has other uses besides, such as a groundsheet or a lean-to emergency shelter. If you don't want to carry extra rain gear, be sure to have a change of clothes in the car so that you won't have to drive home in wet clothing.

Don't forget a toque and gloves. They should be the first things you put on if you feel chilly. If the head, neck and extremities are warm, the rest of the body stays warm. On summer hikes a sun hat and sunglasses are indispensable.

DAYPACKS AND WHAT TO PUT IN THEM

All you will need for a one-day hike is a small daypack. Most are made of nylon, weigh only a few ounces and fasten with a zipper or drawstring. Choose one with outside pockets and padded shoulder straps. A waist strap keeps the pack from shifting if you need to scramble.

Pack your bag carefully with comfort in mind. Light, bulky stuff goes in first with heavier things on top, to keep the weight as high as possible. Keep bumpy objects to the front away from your back, and place the little things you want handy in the outside pockets. Wear the pack high on your shoulders, never sagging in the small of your back, and you will soon forget you are carrying it.

The following items are considered basic equipment for an all-day hike in the wilderness:

Jacket
Toque and gloves
Spare sweater and socks
Rain gear
Spare bootlaces
Lunch and some extra food
Water
Map and compass
Flashlight
Waterproof matches
Candle
Knife
Whistle
Toilet paper
Large plastic bag or emergency space blanket
First-aid kit containing:
    Insect repellent
    Aspirin
    Antiseptic cream
    Adhesive bandage strips
    Roll of 1-inch adhesive tape
    Gauze dressing pads
    Elastic bandage
    Scissors and tweezers
    Moleskin
    Sunscreen
    Tick pliers

The following notes are intended as a guide to the beginning hiker, or the visitor to this area, as to what to expect on hikes at different times of year.

SPRING HIKES

Spring is a tantalizing season for the Vancouver hiker. The first warm days lure us into the hills, where we find, alas, that trails are muddy and strangled with winter's debris and creeks are rushing and swollen. Most daunting of all, at around 750 m (2500 feet) occasional snow patches turn into impassable fields of soft, thawing snow topped with an icy crust that may or may not bear our weight. Moreover, these are conditions that could cause an avalanche.

Because in spring the hiking urge is strong and many people want more demanding expeditions to prepare themselves for summer's alpine hikes, we suggest longer rather than higher walks until the end of May.

The Baden-Powell Trail, made by the Boy Scouts in 1971 as a centennial project, is used widely in this book. Although the entire 40-kilometre (25-mile) trail running along the mountains of the North Shore from Deep Cove to Horseshoe Bay visits various summits on its way, those sections at lower elevations are suitable for spring hiking. Farther afield, some of the Fraser Valley hikes are accessible now and should satisfy the spirit of adventure whilst keeping you below the snow line.

This time of year really tests one's skill in weather predicting, and what to wear can be perplexing. Some spring days are downright hot, and lightweight pants and shirt will feel just right. But remember that the weather can change; on a wilderness hike, you may be out there for several hours.

This may be the season of wet feet, but it is also the season of spring flowers. Those first trilliums and violets you find make up for the inhospitable trails. Bunchberry, fringe cup and star-flowered Solomon's seal all come forth bravely; wild ginger flowers hide beneath their heart-shaped leaves; fiddleheads unfurl. Even those boggy hollows that suck at your boot tops are resplendent with green and gold skunk cabbage.

Besides the sound of running water, the drumming of the ruffed grouse is a familiar accompaniment to a spring hike. This mysterious sound, sometimes mistaken for a distant engine, is made by the quick fluttering motion of the male's wings as he stands upon his drumming log. The females quite rightly find this muffled drum roll exciting. More startling to the hiker is the clatter and whirr of wings when a disturbed grouse bursts into the air and flies across the path.

SUMMER AND FALL HIKES

The months of July, August and September are the zenith of the hiker's year. At this time, even the beginner can enjoy alpine hiking not far from Vancouver.

One word of caution—do not attempt any mountain hike in bad weather. Choose a settled, sunny spell, if possible, and even then, in the mountains, watch the weather constantly. The visibility and the temperature can change in a few minutes when cloud comes down. By September, squalls can bring fresh snow at higher elevations, blotting out surroundings, obliterating trails and numbing summer-clad hikers in minutes.

By June, if you are hiking on good days, pants and a shirt topped with a sleeveless wool or down vest should suffice. The long-sleeved sweater goes into your pack, along with the anorak, woolen toque and squashable sun hat. (This combination might sound odd, but in the mountains you could need both hats on the same day.) If you like to hike in shorts, carry long pants in your pack in case of bothersome insects or a change in temperature.

It is a good idea to take an extra supply of high-energy nibbling food on these longer hiking days. Carry plenty of water, especially if the weather is hot. Remember, too, that a slower pace and more frequent rest stops are called for when hiking at higher altitudes. It has always been one goal of hikers to get above the timberline. The thrill begins as tall trees give way to stunted trees, patches of heath or a stony fell. Views of neighbouring peaks widen into views of other mountain ranges.

Alpine meadows are especially attractive, and the beginner soon discovers that they are not all alike. As well as the "seep" meadows that grow mimulus, lupine, hellebore, mountain valerian and orchids, there are drier meadows where fleabane and Indian paintbrush thrive. Open ridges are carpeted with "cushion" plants, such as saxifrage, dwarf phlox and moss campion.

In alpine country, you are almost sure to see marmots, pikas and grey jays. The jays would be hard to miss; they accompany the hiker through the forest with complaining and derisive cries, and at lunch time swoop down with a soft flutter of wings to share your sandwich. Less saucy but just as entertaining are the marmots, large members of the woodchuck family, who live in colonies on high boulder slopes and rock slides. At your approach, scouts give piercing whistles to warn their clan. The marmots' days in the sun are very few; for nine months of the year, they hibernate beneath the snow in a sleep that is close to death.

It is not so with the pika, or rock rabbit, who bustles around under the snow all winter. These industrious creatures cut bundles of grass and plants during late summer and set them out to cure in the sun. You may notice these small haystacks outside rocky crevices, but the farmer himself is not so easy to spot.

Beyond the flowers and the marmots, you come to the edge of that other world—the region of perpetual snow. At Upper Joffre Lake, for example, you are close to the Matier Glacier. Glaciers are moving rivers of ice formed by compacted snow and forced by gravity, and the weight above, to slide downward over basic bedrock. As the glacier flows, it carries with it chunks of rock from its path, which, in turn, loosen and scoop up more stones and rock. Terminal and lateral moraines are formed when these rocks and grits are deposited at the glacier's snout and sides under the thawing process. The U-shaped valleys formed by the scouring action of moving glaciers can be seen in parts of the world that were once under an ice sheet. Original river beds are often deepened, leaving hanging valleys and waterfalls.

In late September and October come some of the best hiking days of the year. Flowers have turned to seed heads, and berries take their place; black huckleberry, blueberry and bearberry all appear at this time. The hillsides are splashed with crimson, gold and scarlet as the first frosts touch the leaves of ground shrubs.

Hot sun, cool air, dry trails—hiking can't get any better than this.

WINTER HIKES

November to February—certainly now is the time for those invigorating dyke walks or a brisk tramp around a city park. You will find that many of the hikes in this book are designated "Good all year" or "Good most of the year," making use of forest and farmland and disused logging roads. Many sections of the estimable Trans Canada Trail are fine for winter hiking.

Remember, too, that a Vancouver winter traditionally includes mild spells, and most rainy days look worse through the window than they are when you venture out. So why not put on your rain gear and get out for an hour or two? Even a short hike will promote a feeling of well-being. Another good idea is to carry a light, waterproof pad for sitting on. Take along a hot drink, choose a sheltered spot and you are all set to enjoy the delights of a winter picnic.

Bird watching can be one of the pleasures of a winter outing. The Fraser estuary is an important wintering area for thousands of migratory ducks, geese and shorebirds. Herons, hawks and owls hunt over the fields and shore, whereas wrens, chickadees, juncos and woodpeckers are some of the winter residents of our woodlands.

Underfoot in the forest, ferns and mosses can be studied, and mushrooms and other fungi admired in all their bizarre and beautiful forms.

Snow and mud on the trail reveal the comings and goings of wildlife. You should be able to spot the cloven hoofprints of deer wherever there is browse, and the raccoon's distinctive prints with five toes on both front and hind feet. Fox and coyote make doglike prints, the fox's pad being smaller and appearing in a string-straight line. The beaver's tracks show webbed hind feet and broad tail marks between the prints.

Why miss out on winter hiking, when there is so much to see and enjoy?

You are equipped with boots, your daypack and some comfortable clothes, and you are ready to get out there. What you do next will probably determine whether or not you become a hiker. No matter how enthusiastic you are now about getting some exercise or discovering the wilderness, *you will only go on walking if you enjoy it.*

A beginner should approach the wilderness in easy stages. This is not the time to go off with the local club for a five-hour tramp; a bad experience now may put you off for life. Choose an easy hike, and let it be a pleasure, not an endurance test. We all know how to walk (and more about that in a moment), but seldom-used muscles can complain and rob us of enjoyment.

Setting out on a walk is setting out on a mini-holiday. You are a free spirit, unreachable by the everyday world, aware only of here and now. There is time to see, hear, touch and smell. In our seasonal notes and trail descriptions we mention things of interest—the social or geological history of the region, the plant and animal life—but the real discoveries are up to you. It's your walk.

No one enjoys walking in a drenching rain, but a showery day need not put you off. You can dress for it, choose your hike accordingly and learn to enjoy the seasons' different faces.

If you plan to share your hiking with someone—and on wilderness and mountain hikes you should not hike alone—be sure that the person is compatible and shares your energy level. Avoid dragging along a reluctant partner; and leave behind the chatterer, however dear a friend, for he or she will steal all your attention from the walk.

Respect the wilderness and get to know it. The countryside is neither friendly nor hostile; you will feel safe and at home there according to how well you understand its nature.

Some wilderness areas are surprisingly fragile, even in this rugged province, and those who use the wilderness have the responsibility for taking care of it. Cutting corners can obliterate trails that other wilderness lovers have made for you to enjoy. Alpine areas,

Rest stop

especially, are easily destroyed. Plants have a short season in which to complete their growing cycle and must also fight for soil and moisture. Restrain yourself from removing plant life; stay on the trails.

Respect your fellow hiker, too. Pack out every scrap of litter.

BEFORE SETTING OUT

Choose the right hike: The walks and hikes in this book have been graded as to skill and stamina required. Start at your own level. Read the information at the beginning of the hike you select. Note the recommended time of year. Know how long the round trip will take you. Know what kind of terrain to expect and what the elevation gain is. Consider the particular needs of your walk, and pack your daypack accordingly. Of course, be sure to take the basics, but resist throwing in everything else "in case."

You may want to look up beforehand any plants or geological features mentioned or expand upon the historical notes.

Pack a lunch: Even if you are only planning to be out for an hour or two, take along a snack—it will add to the enjoyment of your walk—but keep it simple. A sandwich, a hard-boiled egg and some fruit, together with water or a thermos of hot drink in winter is all you should need, plus some nuts or dried fruit to keep up your energy en route.

Start early: If possible, plan to start early in the day. By giving the best of your energy to your walk, you will gain the most enjoyment, as well as cut the chances of mishap. In summer, especially, climbing should be done before the noon heat so that fatigue is lessened, there will be time for a rest at your destination and the return journey will be leisurely and therefore safer than if you were hurrying, and you won't be tempted to try shortcuts which might lead to your getting lost or benighted.

Leave word: Before you leave home, tell someone where you are going and when you expect to be back. You don't expect to get lost or hurt, but if the unforeseeable should happen, others can help you more quickly if you have left word of your whereabouts.

Getting lost before you reach the trail is never a good way to start the day! If you're using public transit, be sure the bus, SkyTrain or West Coast Express is running in the direction you are going and at the time you want to go. Take along a city map and this book.

GOOD WALKING TECHNIQUES

Walking is as natural as breathing. Our weight distribution, flexible spine and arched feet are engineered for walking. Given a chance, the mechanism performs beautifully. The more we walk, the better we are able to do so, but it helps to unlearn bad walking habits, too.

Striding: Try to keep your toes pointing straight forward. Walking with turned-out toes causes fatigue and leads to dropped arches, backache and short steps. Walking pigeon-toed puts a strain on the knees.

Lengthening the stride corrects most walking faults; that extra swing of the leg seems to help the entire body. Your spine straightens, supporting your frame; your stomach muscles tighten, letting your hips slide forward under your torso; and your arms swing to your body's rhythm, relaxing your shoulders as your head comes up of its own accord. Your body has now taken over and you are walking naturally.

Starting off: It is a good idea to begin slowly. Be casual, gaze around at your surroundings, give your body a chance to warm up, and quite soon you will find your natural pace taking over. If, however, you charge quickly up the trail at the start, you will soon have to stop to get your breath, and your body, which was warming up, now cools down again, delaying the hitting of your natural pace.

Climbing: Slow down a bit and take shorter steps. There is no harm in zigzagging up a trail, leaning forward, hooking your hands in your rucksack straps or doing anything else that makes you feel comfortable, but try to keep going if you possibly can—the rhythm of progress will reinforce your will, and soon you will look up to find that the slope has been conquered.

Taking breaks: A five-minute breather every half hour is about right for most people. Sit, or lean, during your rest stops. Rather than take off your pack, simply support it against a tree or log. Nibble a snack if you like; observe your surroundings. Enjoy the rest break, but don't take more than five or six minutes—if you do, starting up again can be hard.

Stopping for lunch: This is the time when you should relax more fully. Choose your spot carefully. Make yourself comfortable. When you sit down to eat, put on that extra sweater even if you feel warm. By conserving body heat then, you are conserving energy. If you wait until you start to shiver, all your precious heat/energy will have leaked away and you will have to work twice as hard when you start walking again to generate more. After you have finished eating, rest for a few minutes or explore the area before getting back on the trail.

Using walking sticks: For many of the hikes in this book, a walking stick or Nordic pole would be in order for those who like them, though they can be in the way if you need your hands to scramble up steep slopes. You will have to find out for yourself whether or not to carry one.

COPING

No matter how well prepared you are, during your first hikes you will probably meet some minor difficulties on the trail. Knowing how to cope will keep these setbacks from spoiling your enjoyment. If you experience any of the following sensations, your body is trying to tell you something. Listen, and do something about it right away.

You feel faint soon after starting: You are probably wearing too many clothes—the most common fault of beginners. Even mild exercise, such as walking, increases body heat several degrees. Strip off that extra sweater and let the air get to your skin. Parkas and anoraks should only be worn if it is raining or there is a freezing wind.

Your thighs ache: You are going uphill too fast. Slow down and try taking shorter steps.

Your back aches: Try tightening the straps of your pack to get the weight higher on your back. If necessary, repack it to get bumpy objects off your spine. Think about posture, too. Have you slumped into a gorilla crouch?

Your feet are getting sore: At the first hint of soreness, get a plaster or moleskin over that patch of red skin.

You experience shortness of breath: You are probably fatigued or becoming exhausted. Take a rest break. Afterwards, walk or climb more slowly at a pace that is comfortable for you.

You have a "stitch": You are trying to go too fast. Perhaps you started too soon after lunch. Slow down, or stop and rest until it goes.

You have a cramp: You may be dehydrated—drink some water.

You feel chilled: Put on your hat and gloves to counteract the chilled feeling that creeps in after a rest stop or when you are tired. On long hikes, nibbling nuts or raisins will keep your heat/energy level up.

You don't think you can keep going: If something is really hurting, go slowly for a while and take more frequent, short rest stops. Pain crushes the spirit and causes you to start believing that you can't go on. Try not to think ahead too much—how far you have to go, how many hours of walking. Concentrate instead on this bit of trail, the sunlight slanting through the trees here, this rock, that twisted root, the footsteps you are taking now. Some people find it easier to be in the lead when they are tired.

OTHER ANNOYANCES

The children keep stopping: You are probably attempting too ambitious a hike for them. Very young children can't see the point of hiking; they would rather stop and play. If you want to get them interested in hiking, break them in gently with short, leisurely outings. If you have to nag them, they will never take to it.

The older children keep dashing ahead: This is a serious problem. Restrain them. It takes only moments for children to disappear around a bend in the trail. If they are out of sight, someone else may go off the trail looking for them and all become lost.

People keep getting left behind: Wait for them. The rule should be: If one stops, everyone waits.

You run out of trail markers or trail: Stop. Go back to the last marker you saw and make a few short forays in different directions until you pick up the markers again. After each unsuccessful attempt, return to the known point. Unless otherwise stated, all of the hikes in this book follow defined trails that use signs, markers and/or a well-trodden footbed to show the way.

COURTESY ON THE TRAIL

It is not only good sense but also good manners to call a warning if you discover a hazard, such as a loose rock or a slippery log. Try not to let branches flip back onto others. Better yet, keep space between yourself and the next person. Wisdom dictates that hikers take care of each other in the wilderness; carrying out a casualty can be a tough job.

This chapter covers some aspects of hiking that cannot always be avoided. Preparedness, some basic knowledge, proper equipment and the resilient human spirit are all needed to cope with wilderness hazards.

HAZARDS OF TERRAIN

Expect some bad terrain; don't underrate it. Above all, *don't hurry*.

Negotiating roots: Roots that criss-cross the trail can be slippery, especially when wet. Avoid stepping on them, if possible; get them under your instep, if not.

Crossing creeks: Never underestimate the force of moving water. A stick or pole is helpful when wading through creeks; place it on the upstream side, keep it slanted, walk past and below it, then repeat the manoeuvre at each step. Never wade facing downstream or the water may cause your legs to buckle. Cross stepping stones very carefully. A mad dash from boulder to boulder invites injury that will be far more inconvenient than wet feet.

Crossing rock slides: Even after centuries in one place, boulders that have broken away from a mountain are still only poised, jammed against one another. They are even more treacherous when covered with moss, snow or ice. When a trail crosses a boulder slope, move slowly, testing each step. If a rock moves, shout a warning to others and get out of the way as quickly as you can.

Scrambling over rocks: Check each handhold before using it. Get the toe of your boot onto good footholds. If facing forward while descending makes you uneasy, go down backward.

WEATHER HAZARDS

You find snow on the trail: Patches of old, hard snow are usually fine for walking on and need not present a hazard. Wet, thawing snow is difficult underfoot. When ruts and holes develop and water runs beneath the snow, beware. To sink suddenly up to your waist in cold wetness is never funny. Use that trail when the thaw is over.

Resting with mosquito net

A snowstorm blows up: It is usually best to turn back—a trail is soon hidden by snow. If you are on an open ridge and cloud begins to swirl around you, retreat immediately to where the trail is marked and sheltered. In the mountains, the drop in temperature that cloud brings is a serious hazard to the hiker. (See the section on "Coping with hypothermia" later in this chapter.)

Lightning strikes: Electrical storms are not frequent in this area, but when lightning occurs, it is best to take precautions. Avoid places where your head is likely to be the highest point for miles around. If you are out in the open, crouch or lie down. Do not shelter under the highest object in the vicinity. You are safer in the woods than in the open, but never shelter under one lone tree.

You run out of daylight: Darkness must be regarded as a weather hazard to the hiker. Start early and know how much daylight is available for your hike. Leave word with someone as to where you will be hiking and the time you intend to return. If darkness does catch you in the wilderness, it is better to stay out overnight than try to follow a rough, unlighted trail. (See the section on "Spending the night out" later in this chapter.)

You encounter extreme heat: This is only a hazard if you have not taken proper precautions. Guard against sunstroke and sunburn by covering up; wear long sleeves and long trousers, a sun hat or visor, sunglasses, a tested sunscreen lotion. A person suffering from overexposure will have a flushed face and hot, dry skin. Have the victim sit in a cool place and sip some water. Put cold packs on face, neck and arms.

Guard against heat exhaustion by not overdoing it when the weather is hot and by wearing loose clothing.

CREATURE HAZARDS

Mosquitoes, blackflies and other insects: These pests are not always present, but be prepared for them, especially in damp areas from early May through September. In fact, never go hiking without insect repellent in your pack. The stick kind is handy; keep reapplying. Long sleeves and trousers minimize the nuisance, and, to insects, lighter-coloured clothes seem to be less appealing than dark ones. Be aware that bees and wasps are active in summer and early fall. They may nest in trees and bushes and in old logs and stumps. In the case of a bee sting, remove the stinger with tweezers (wasps do not have a barbed stinger) and apply a cold, damp cloth to relieve any swelling.

Ticks: Like lightning, ticks are rarely encountered but require a bit of special knowledge. They may drop onto you from overhanging bushes or from long grass. Insect repellent generally deters them, but if a persistent tick attaches itself to you, do not try to brush it off; instead, use tick pliers to pull it straight out, being careful not to crush it. A tick absorbs oxygen through its body, so a dab of grease or oil may cause it to withdraw and drop off. If these attempts fail, have a doctor remove it as soon as possible.

Snakes: There are no poisonous snakes in the areas described in this book.

Bears: Bears do inhabit the country around Vancouver but are not often seen. They avoid contact with humans for good reasons of their own. However, bears are unpredictable and potentially dangerous. If you see one, stay calm. Talk in a low, soothing voice. Keep still for a moment to let the bear see you properly—these animals are short-sighted—then calmly proceed or retreat, whichever seems the wisest. Never approach a bear, and never turn and run or it may give chase. Be especially alert around berry patches and stream banks. If you see evidence of bears, such as droppings or fresh tracks, singing or raising your voice will announce your presence. Some hikers attach bells to their packs to warn bears of their approach.

SURVIVAL

It's a good idea to have some basic first-aid training. St. John Ambulance offers courses, as do several other organizations specializing in wilderness first aid. Make sure, too, that anyone in your group with a special medical condition carries the necessary medication or equipment. Being lost, benighted or hurt while you are hiking in the wilderness are situations that become a matter of survival. First, there will be some decisions to make, so it is important to get a grip on your thinking. Don't panic. Think. When everybody is calm, set to work and do what you can.

What to do if someone is injured: Any injury is accompanied by some degree of shock. Make the casualty as comfortable as possible. Provide warmth and a drink, if needed, and let the person rest a moment.

If there is a broken bone, you should immobilize the limb. Make splints out of whatever is handy, pad them with spare clothing and fasten them to the injured limb. A broken arm can be strapped to the body.

A sprained ankle should be elevated and a firm bandage applied. If possible, keep wetting the bandage with cold water. If the patient must walk, put on the boot soon or swelling may make it impossible.

When everyone is rested, the walking wounded can be helped down the trail. A person with a broken leg will have to be carried. If you are able to use a cell phone to contact a rescue team, give the place of the accident (a map reference is best), the time and the injuries. If this is not possible, someone will have to go for help.

Going for help: If there are four people—the ideal number for wilderness hiking—one stays with the casualty, two go for help. They should leave food, water and extra clothing with the injured person and, before setting off, should make a note of the place and details of the accident. Above all, those who go for help must travel safely and arrive in good enough shape to guide the rescuers back.

Coping with hypothermia: This condition heads the list of hikers' hazards. When the inner part of your body—your own central heating plant—gets too cold, your system stops functioning. Hypothermia can occur anywhere and at any time that the air temperature drops low enough to reduce inner body temperature. *It doesn't have to be below freezing.* Cold, wet and wind can chill the body faster than it can produce heat. Improper clothing, lack of food and fatigue all contribute to hypothermia.

Because the onset of hypothermia blunts a person's ability to think, a victim may not realize what is happening. Group members should keep an eye on each other for signs of fatigue and discomfort. If a member of the party goes pale and quiet, and begins to shiver or stumble, act quickly. Get the victim out of the cold, wind or rain. Remove wet clothing and replace with dry things. Wrap the person in a space blanket or heap everybody's spare clothes and gear beneath and around the victim's body to prevent further loss of body heat. Direct body heat from another person can also be helpful. If the victim is semi-conscious, keep him or her awake, giving warm drinks and a little food, if possible. Let the person rest before starting again.

Hypothermia can be fatal, but almost always it could have been prevented by obeying the elementary rules for hikers.

What to do if you are lost: First, sit down and rest. There is a good chance you are not lost at all but merely tired and confused. Think. Try to recall how you got where you are. In which direction did you wander? Where was the sun? What landmarks had you seen? Take time to consider, and with the aid of your map, compass and memory, decide on the direction you need to go to find the trail. Mark your path with arrows or stones. Do not go too far, but return to your starting point, and set off in another direction, again marking your way. Never wander aimlessly through the bush. With the aid of your compass, keep a steady course on each excursion and you are more than likely to strike your familiar trail and get back to civilization under your own steam.

If your exploratory attempts are unsuccessful, if you are injured or exhausted, if it is getting dark or the weather is very bad—then you should be prepared to stay put until daylight or until someone finds you. If you carry a cell phone and are able to get a signal, alert someone to your predicament. Stay at, or close to, the place where you first discovered you were lost. Don't make the mistake of thinking that following a creek downhill will lead you to safety. Mountain rescue teams point out that in our rugged terrain, creeks usually lead to drop-offs and canyons, where you are more likely to be injured and where it is more difficult to hear searchers' voices.

Spending the night out: First you must set about finding, or making, a shelter. Get out of the wind; use trees, boulders, a cave or a sheltered spot behind big logs. You can make a shelter by propping branches against a rock or tree to form a framework, then thatching it with evergreen boughs. Use the materials at hand, but avoid cutting live wood unnecessarily.

Next, look for firewood. Even in wet weather, dry material can usually be found inside hollow logs. As well as providing heat, your fire will act as a smoke signal for those searching for you. Look for water; it is important not to become dehydrated. You can manage quite a long time without food, but if you decide to eat plants or berries, eat only those you know. Put on all your clothing and huddle together for warmth. You will survive the night and someone will be looking for you.

> TRAIL INFORMATION

Although the hikes in this guide might be regarded as "easy" by an expert hiker, "easy" can mean different things to a beginner, to an elderly walker or to a family with small children. Therefore, considering distance, elevation gain and terrain in relation to each other, and with the non-expert in mind, we have classified each hike as "easy," "moderately easy" or "moderately difficult." Together with maps and trail descriptions, these classifications should help the reader to choose the hike that has sufficient challenge and interest but is not beyond his or her ability to enjoy.

In the trail descriptions, our estimated hiking time allows for an easier pace than that used by experts. A lunch break is *not* included in the hiking time. Rough distances for the hikes are given in kilometres and miles. Elevation gain of less than 150 m (500 feet) is not always noted.

The hikes are accompanied by simple trail maps to supplement the text, and under normal conditions, these will be an adequate guide. In addition, we recommend that wilderness hikers carry and know how to use a topographical map and a compass. As well as being a safety guide—in the wilderness it may be vitally important to be able to orientate yourself—the detailed map will increase the interest of your hike, enabling you to identify mountains, rivers and other landmarks. A good source of topographical and recreational maps is International Travel Maps and Books, 12300 Bridgeport Road, Richmond, B.C., v6v 1J5.

For clarity, hikes that use old, disused logging roads have been shown on the maps as trails. However, where such an old road provides a useful landmark for the hiker, it is shown as a logging road.

All the hikes have been surveyed within the two years prior to, first printing of this edition. However, trails are subject to change for various reasons, such as rerouting because of construction or logging operations, skiing activities, occasional vandalism or weather conditions, which can cause washouts and obstructions. Expect occasional changes in the route; follow markers.

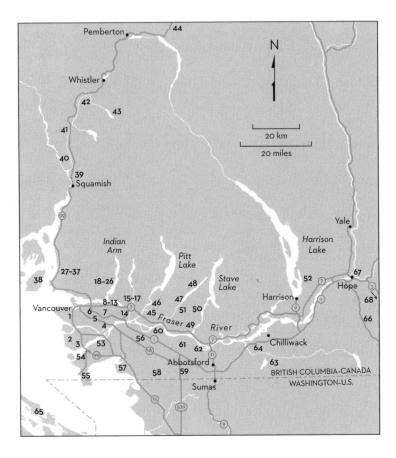

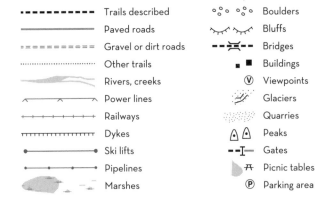

KEY TO MAPS

PACIFIC SPIRIT
REGIONAL PARK

Round trip 6 km (3³/₄ miles)

Allow 2 hours

Good all year

FAMILY HIKE

EASY

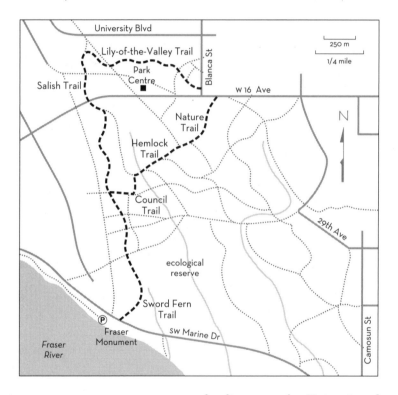

THIS UNIQUE REGIONAL park adjacent to the University of British Columbia provides more than 50 km (31 miles) of trails for walking and many more designated for cyclists and horseback riders. It is a shared and carefully preserved wilderness area, comprising mixed and coniferous forest, ancient bog and miles of foreshore. The region is a habitat for some uncommon plants as well as for

View from Simon Fraser monument

songbirds, owls, eagles, squirrels, raccoons, otters, coyotes and deer. And all this is a mere 15-minute drive from the centre of Vancouver.

The 6-km (3¾-mile) circuit described here takes advantage of two trails reserved for pedestrians only and is part of a walking route dedicated to Vancouver resident Iva Mann, in recognition of her efforts toward the preservation of the University Endowment Lands as a park.

> A WORD OF ADVICE Although trail names are shown on signposts along the way, if you're tempted to explore and diverge from the route described, you'll need a park map to guide you through the maze of trails criss-crossing the area. (Maps are available from the Park Centre on West 16th Avenue just west of Blanca Street and from kiosks at several park entrances, including one at the foot of Camosun Street on S.W. Marine Drive.)

> GETTING THERE The starting point for this outing is the parking area at the Simon Fraser monument on S.W. Marine Drive, about 2 km (1¼ miles) west of the junction of Camosun Street and S.W. Marine Drive.

This starting point may not be accessible by public transit. You could take the #33 bus from King Edward Station and alight at

16th Avenue and Blanca Street and join the hiking route at midpoint. For up-to-date information, contact TransLink at 604-953-3333 or visit their website at translink.ca.

> THE TRAIL After reading of Simon Fraser's arrival on Point Grey in 1808 and looking down upon the booming grounds and the delta of the Fraser River's north arm, cross S.W. Marine from the eastern end of the parking lot and enter the forest on Sword Fern Trail.

At first, boardwalks carry you over marshy ground, tall cedars towering overhead. Proceeding northward through second-growth forest—the giant Douglas-firs of the southern slope of Point Grey fell to the axe in the 1880s—you skirt an ecological reserve (not open to the public) before crossing several multi-use trails. Fungi flourish on the forest floor and, of course, sword fern, among others.

After about a half hour's walking, a left turn onto Salish Trail brings you to West 16th Avenue, which you must cross. Continue on Salish, cross Heron Trail and watch for the signpost for Lily of the Valley Trail. Go right here and follow the winding path through mixed deciduous and coniferous forest, embroidered with wildflowers in spring and summer. After crossing Cleveland (which leads to the Park Centre), Lily of the Valley passes through an area of huge cedar stumps and ancient nurse logs.

At the next trail junction, switch to Vine Maple and follow this out to Blanca Street. Turn right to re-cross West 16th Avenue and walk east along the verge for a few metres to the start of Nature Trail. This is a multi-use trail, so be prepared for cyclists.

Now your route plunges you into sombre coniferous forest where tall, straight firs and hemlocks form a canopy overhead. Passing Deer Fern and Cleveland Trails, keep right when you come to Hemlock and right again on Salish Trail to cross Cutthroat Creek on the bridge. This modest stream, rescued by community efforts from destruction, is now a spawning ground for salmon and home to tiny, endangered cutthroat trout.

A few metres beyond the creek, go left on Iron Knee. Next, a right turn on Council Trail will soon bring you back to Sword Fern, along which you retrace your steps southward to your starting point.

TERRA NOVA

Round trip 5 km (3 miles)
Allow 2 hours
Good all year

Wheelchair accessible West
Dyke Trail and Middle Arm Trail
FAMILY HIKE
EASY

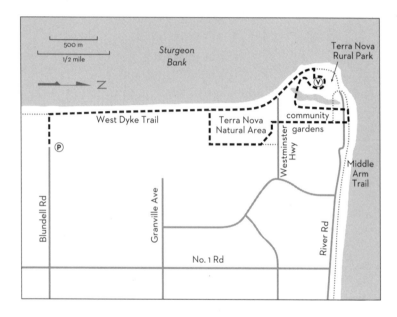

RICHMOND'S POPULAR WEST Dyke Trail from Steveston to Terra Nova has much to offer year round. Heading north from one of the dyke access points—the western foot of Blundell Road works well for the family outing described here—you have the tidal marshes of Sturgeon Bank offshore and a view of the North Shore Mountains ahead. You'll circumnavigate an area of field habitat where you may spot pheasants, hawks and owls; you can spend time examining the vegetable plots of a community garden where Richmond schoolchildren learn to plant, tend and cook their produce. A grandstand view of airport activity awaits those who rest or picnic by

Parson House

the Fraser River, and paths through land that was once the domain of a farming and fishing community lend a feeling of being out in the country.

> **GETTING THERE** From No. 2 or No. 3 Road in Richmond, turn west on Blundell Road and drive to its end, where there is roadside parking and access to the dyke path.

> **THE TRAIL** Set off northward along the dyke. Inland, watch for an eagles' nest built in the fork of a tree bordering Quilchena golf course. On the seaward side, hawks, herons and distant freighters go about their business. After about 1 km (½ mile), branch off to the right into Terra Nova Natural Area. The rescue and preservation of this field habitat is described at the beginning of the perimeter trail. As you approach Westminster Highway, take the boardwalk to the left and continue westward along the path until you are opposite the red barn. Cross the road here and walk north between the garden plots of vegetables and flowers. As you continue northward from the gardens, set your sights on the yellow building straight ahead.

This is Parson House, whose interesting history and ownership is described on the notice board.

Ignoring for the moment those alluring trails to the left, cross River Road to join the Middle Arm Trail, where benches and picnic tables invite a pause. Cyclists and joggers pedal and pound the dyke path, seaplanes take off from the river, aircraft from all over the world arrive at and depart from Vancouver International Airport on Sea Island opposite. When you've had enough of the busy scene, you can explore the newly developed Terra Nova Rural Area.

Start by taking the path opposite the washroom building, heading inland beneath tall Douglas-firs. Follow the paths and boardwalk around the restored slough; try out one of the innovative benches; climb the gravel path to the summit of the man-made hill for an unusual view of Richmond and Sturgeon Bank. Closer at hand, you'll see a row of horse chestnut trees (glorious in fall) and the remains of wooden fences that tell of long-gone farms. Rejoin the West Dyke Trail by the obvious access below and tramp the homeward stretch to Blundell.

3

Richmond

SOUTH DYKE TRAIL

Round trip 7.2 km (4½ miles)
Allow 2 hours
Good all year

Wheelchair accessible from No. 3
Rd. to London Farm
FAMILY HIKE
EASY

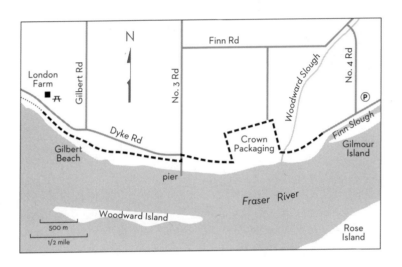

PART OF THE lengthy South Dyke Trail to Steveston, this interesting walk beside the south arm of the Fraser River is a gift for a
winter day when other trails are wet or muddy. Beginning from the
tidal community of Finn Slough, squeezed between the dyke and
Gilmour Island (sometimes known as Whitworth Island), you'll see
both beached and working fishing boats in the channel, sheds and
houses built on stilts and the one-time Dinner Plate Island School.
Information about this 1890s Finnish fishing community is provided near the wooden drawbridge.

A turnaround point at the restored London Heritage Farm offers
additional historical interest. The farmhouse, tea room and gift shop
are open most weekend afternoons and in summer from Wednesday
through Sunday, 12 to 5 PM. Entrance is by donation.

Finn Slough

Between these two attractions, there are driftwood beaches to explore; bustling river traffic to watch; and seals, gulls and diving ducks to catch your eye.

> GETTING THERE Leave Highway 99 at exit 32 in Richmond and drive west on Steveston Highway. Turn left on No. 5 Road and right on Dyke Road. Turn right on No. 4 Road and park on the roadside before crossing the railway.

> THE TRAIL Set off westward along Dyke Road beside Finn Slough's funky residences. At the end of the road, go through the gate and continue along the dyke, past the outlet of Woodward Slough, until you are forced to circumnavigate the Crown Packaging plant. Once back to the riverbank, the area opens out into a dog off-leash park, at the end of which is a sport fishing pier. From here you follow the roadside trail with its wide views of the river and Westham Island opposite.

After passing Gilbert Beach, you soon arrive at London Farm. Here you might choose to visit the restored farmhouse, stroll around the gardens and allotments or examine some farm machinery from bygone days. Picnic tables invite a rest before retracing your steps to Finn Slough. If you've chosen a clear day for this outing, Mount Baker's snowy peaks to the south will enhance the homeward stretch.

4

Burnaby

FRASER FORESHORE PARK

Round trip 8 km (5 miles)   Good all year

Allow 3 hours   **EASY**

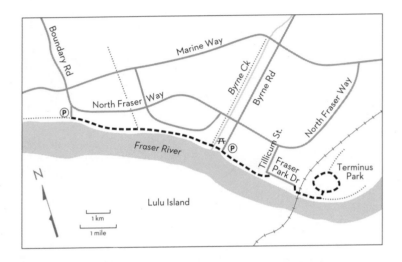

FROM THIS SHORELINE trail along the north arm of the Fraser River in southwest Burnaby you'll see the tugboats, barges and log booms of a working river—and more. Fringed with wild roses, thimbleberry and snowberry bushes, the path crosses Byrne Creek as it nears the hub of the park at the foot of Byrne Road. In 1893, the original Byrne Creek was channelled into a ditch to allow logging companies to float their logs down to the Fraser on the way to sawmills in New Westminster. At the eastern end of Fraser Foreshore Trail is Terminus Park, where wetland has been rescued from industry; sloughs and ponds have been created to aid salmon spawning and fields preserved for wildlife.

> TRY THIS WALK IN ANY SEASON Spring for the scent of cottonwoods, summer for songbirds and winter for a varied walk when mountain trails are under snow. Note, too, that the riverside trail has now been extended west of Boundary Road.

Bridge over Byrne Creek

> **GETTING THERE** Drive south on Boundary Road in Burnaby and park at the road's end near the river.

This starting point is accessible by public transit. Take the #116 bus from Metrotown Station or Edmonds Station and alight at North Fraser Way and Boundary Road. For up-to-date information, contact TransLink at 604-953-3333 or visit their website at translink.ca.

> **THE TRAIL** Set off eastward along the riverbank, industry to your left, marine traffic and booming grounds to your right. Gulls and cormorants perch on the pilings; sparrows and chickadees, and warblers in summer, dart among the bushes. After crossing an arched bridge over Byrne Creek, you can view the river from a platform—whilst sitting on a Brobdingnagian chair if you wish. As you near the picnic area and playground at the foot of Byrne Road, you enter a grove of black cottonwoods. Watch for woodpeckers and brown creepers working up and down the furrowed bark of these majestic trees.

Continuing upstream from the Byrne Road facilities, you'll come to a wooden pier from where you can look across the water to Lulu Island's River Road on the opposite shore. Soon after this, you must walk along a road for a short distance before proceeding down a gated track to the right and passing beneath the old CN railway bridge with its movable centre span allowing river traffic to pass through.

Now you are entering Terminus Park. Much of this area is closed to the public, but you may turn left and then right to follow a circular pathway that takes you through the restored wetlands. After crossing a bridge, you walk beside an open meadow where poles have been erected to encourage raptors. Back at the beginning of the circular path, you have reached your turnaround point, ready to retrace your outward journey.

DEER LAKE TRAILS

Round trip 8 km (5 miles)   Good all year
Allow 3 hours   **EASY**

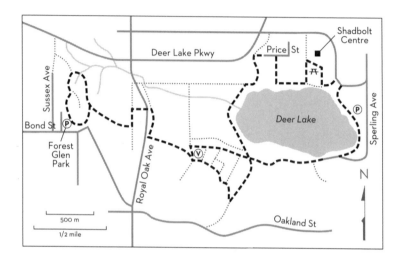

DEER LAKE PARK is home to the Burnaby Village Museum, the
Shadbolt Centre for the Arts and surrounding Century Gardens,
Hart House and other heritage buildings. Trails extending westward
from the lake through land that once belonged to a long-gone peni-
tentiary can be linked with Forest Glen Park and the Sussex Avenue
Bikeway to make a respectable walk in the heart of the city.

The route described embraces forest, meadow and marshland, as
well as some ups and downs with wide views of the city and mountains to the north and east. In winter, the lake is a haven for ducks;
in spring, you'll see barn, cliff and violet-green swallows swooping
over the water. Although the lakeside highlights and facilities make
a fitting destination and turnaround point, by using the map and
honing your navigational skills, you could shorten or lengthen your
walk and enjoy a good tramp in any season.

Going down the Deer Lake

> **GETTING THERE** Leave Highway 1 in Burnaby at exit 29 and drive south on Willingdon Avenue. After crossing Moscrop/Deer Lake Parkway, turn left on Bond Street. Park on Kira Court at the southwest corner of Forest Glen Park.

This starting point can be reached by public transit: Take the Metrotown/Lougheed Station #110 bus and alight on Bond Street near Forest Glen Park. For up-to-date information, contact Trans-Link at 604-953-3333 or visit their website at translink.ca.

> **THE TRAIL** Start by walking downhill on the grass, past the play-ground to a sign: "Deer Lake West Trail." Follow this into the woods, staying left at the first fork but turning right (east) at the next one on a trail leading to a bridge with information panels about wet-land flora and fauna. Continuing now in a southeasterly direction, you'll pass a trail coming from the right (your return route) and will shortly emerge on what used to be Royal Oak Avenue. Walk a few steps downhill and go right to pass beneath the present Royal Oak. Turn right again to climb away from the lowlands. Leaving a wild-life viewing platform for your return and ignoring a flight of steps to

the right, keep choosing the upper trail at subsequent forks, thereby enjoying expansive views to the north and east, until you reach an acute left turn beside a rusty chain-link fence (right goes to Oakland Street).

Follow this ravine trail down toward the lake, turning right when you reach the main trail. Continue eastward, passing beneath a wooden arch and finally stepping out onto a narrow paved road. Go left at the information board, toward the lakeside buildings and beach. Follow the lakeshore by skirting the parking area. After passing below the Hart House Restaurant, you will need to use a short stretch of Dale Avenue in order to cross a creek. Turn left between posts onto a gravel track opposite an entrance to the Burnaby Village Museum. Turn right at the T-junction and head toward the Shadbolt Centre and Century Gardens or walk across the open concert bowl to find a picnic table or a bench to rest on.

When you are ready to leave, head for the lakeshore and dock and follow the boardwalk westward. At its end, you must detour past some houses, turning left when you reach Price Street and left again when you meet the trail heading back toward the lake. A further left turn takes you along the marshy western end of the lake on a boardwalk. At its end, take the second path to the right, along which you continue as far as the ramp to the wildlife viewing platform. Now is your chance to visit this structure and watch for red-tailed hawks and northern harriers over the low-lying fields or songbirds around the pond below.

Leaving the platform by the upper path, you will quickly find yourself at a familiar information board opposite a flight of steps. From this point, you can turn right and retrace your outward route through the Royal Oak underpass to pick up the trail to Forest Glen Park. This time, though, take the first trail ascending left, which brings you out onto a road. Make for the large rock ahead and follow the path across the park to the playground and Kira Court from where you began the day's adventure.

BURNABY LAKE

Round trip 10.5 km (6½ miles)   **Wheelchair accessible** Piper Avenue
Allow 3½ hours   Spit only
Good all year   FAMILY HIKE (Piper Spit area)
                                 EASY

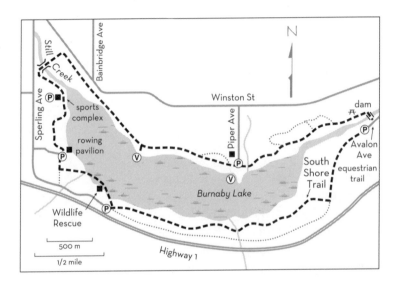

NESTLED IN A low-lying valley and bordered by marshes, Burnaby Lake is a haven for birds, animals and nature lovers. A well-groomed trail encircles the lake, offering more than 10 km (6 miles) of surprisingly peaceful walking, considering the lake's proximity to industry and highway. There is interest at every season of the year, from muskrats to water lilies, fall colours to tracks in the snow.

> GETTING THERE There are three designated entrances to this regional park, as well as some other access points, such as the Rowing Pavilion suggested here.

Leave Highway 1 eastbound at the Sprott Street exit 32, turning left on Sprott Street to cross the highway. Cross Kensington Avenue at the traffic lights and turn right on Sperling then left on Roberts, where signs direct you to the Rowing Pavilion.

Although the starting point cannot be reached by public transit, you could take the Metrotown/Lougheed Station bus #110 to Government Road and Piper Avenue and walk down Piper Avenue to pick up the hiking route. For up-to-date information, contact Trans-Link at 604-953-3333 or visit their website at translink.ca.

> THE TRAIL Set off northward along Pavilion Trail, first through a marshy area, then branching right to pass behind the Burnaby Lake Sports Complex. Shortly after crossing Still Creek, whose peaty brown waters flow into the lake, you begin your journey along the lake's north shore. A spur trail leads to a viewpoint beside the water.

The Piper Avenue entrance to the park, which you approach next, boasts a nature house (open weekends and statutory holidays May to Thanksgiving) and a bird-watching tower, as well as the usual facilities. A boardwalk along Piper Spit provides close-up viewing of waterfowl and a large beaver lodge at its end. Farther ahead, two adjoining loop trails explore the woods.

To continue your circuit of the lake, follow the main trail eastward to the outlet of the Brunette River and the Cariboo Dam. This engineering project not only helps to prevent flooding downstream but also controls the depth of the lake—an important factor affecting the stability of Highway 1. Picnic tables near the dam provide a good lunch spot, particularly as beyond this point traffic noise is a background to your walk.

After crossing over the dam, you will soon arrive at the Avalon Avenue parking lot, where you begin the homeward stretch by joining the equestrian trail for about 800 m (½ mile) until you come to the South Shore Trail branching right. On this you wend your way along the edge of the marsh, assisted at times by boardwalks. After passing behind the Wildlife Rescue Association establishment, you will pick up Pavilion Trail again on your right, thereby returning from whence you started.

BURNABY MOUNTAIN TRAILS

Round trip 8.7 km (5½ miles)   **Allow** 4 hours

High point 300 m (985 feet)   Good most of the year

Elevation gain 270 m (885 feet)   **MODERATELY EASY**

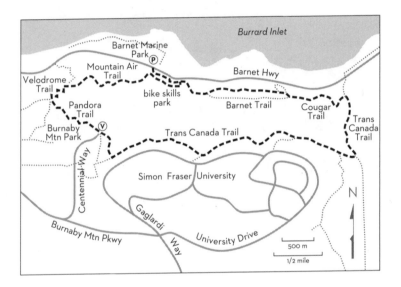

A NETWORK OF forest trails encircles the Simon Fraser University campus atop Burnaby Mountain. Although part of the rugged north slope of the 575-ha (1420-acre) conservation area is out of bounds for safety reasons, the hike described offers the reasonably fit hiker a satisfying circuit on the northern side of the mountain with the bonus of the civilized attractions of Burnaby Mountain Park—a breathtaking viewpoint, Japanese ceremonial totem poles, Horizons Restaurant and a rose garden.

> GETTING THERE Drive east on Hastings Street in Burnaby and turn left on Inlet Drive, which becomes Barnet Highway (Highway 7A). Turn left at the traffic lights into Barnet Marine Park parking lot.

Playground of the Gods

This starting point can be reached by public transit: Take the Vancouver/Port Coquitlam Station bus #160 and alight at the entrance to Barnet Marine Park in the 8300 block of Barnet Highway. For up-to-date information, contact TransLink at 604-953-3333 or visit their website at translink.ca.

> THE TRAIL Cross Barnet Highway at the traffic lights and enter Mountain Air Bike Skills Park. Stay outside the fence and follow the old road as it dips into a hollow then rises beyond a gate with a signpost for Barnet Trail to a transmission line right-of-way. Tramp along this road for about 300 m (330 yards) until you reach Hang Your Hat Trail branching left into the forest. On this winding woodland path, with its streams and bridges, you roughly parallel the transmission line for almost 1 km (½ mile). An optional minor loop to Elephant Ridge offers a partial view of Burrard Inlet.

After rejoining Barnet Trail, you climb to a minor crest. Here, where the powerline heads uphill, you switch to Cougar Trail and descend steeply toward the highway before rising again to a junction with the Trans Canada Trail. Turn right here and brace yourself for a stiff climb. Walk on the right, out of the way of flying cyclists.

After catching your breath at a trail junction with an information kiosk, turn right with the Trans Canada Trail (AKA Joe's Trail) and proceed westward for 2.8 km (1¾ miles), crossing several ravines along the way. Ignore trails branching left leading up to the Simon Fraser University campus. When you reach a fork with a signpost for Pandora Trail, turn right and follow the fence downhill past a playground and rose garden into Burnaby Mountain Park. Here you can enjoy a well-earned break, take in the view of Indian Arm, examine the living sculpture of two cranes and wonder at Kamui Mintara, the Playground of the Gods.

To continue, stay on Pandora Trail as it follows the fence downhill then curves across the lawn below the Japanese poles and descends to a trail junction signposted Gnomes Home. Keep right at this fork and within a few steps you'll see Velodrome Trail branching sharply right. This is your route. As you descend (carefully) down the 500 steps, holding the rope handline, you can thank the Burnaby Parks, Recreation and Cultural Services for this wonderful staircase—an engineering feat that enables you to cope safely with the steep terrain. Turn right when you come to Mountain Air Trail and follow this delightful woodland path back to Bike Skills Park. Cross the parking lot to exit through the gate beside the outhouse. (If you are hiking during the winter months, when the park, and perhaps the gate, is closed, you might have to find a place to squeeze out beside the fence.)

Your circular hike now complete, it only remains to cross the Barnet Highway to your car, but if you still have time and energy to spare, cross the railway overpass into Barnet Marine Park and wind down by taking a stroll along the waterfront on Drummonds Walk.

SHORELINE TRAIL

Round trip 6 km (3³/₄ miles)   FAMILY HIKE
Allow 2 hours   **EASY**
Good all year

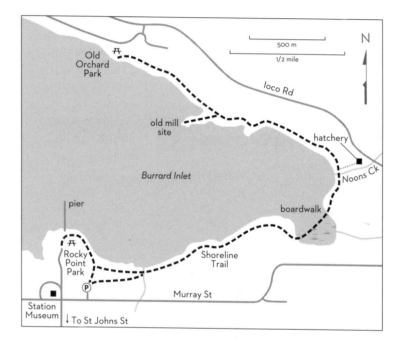

PRESERVATION OF THE waterfront at the head of Burrard Inlet has provided outdoor lovers with an easy 3-km (2-mile) walk of boundless interest. A separate cycle path enhances the pleasure for all. From the boardwalks and viewing platforms, walkers can watch ducks, grebes, gulls and shorebirds at most times of year. Swallows and band-tailed pigeons arrive in spring; summer brings humming-birds, warblers and vireos. In fall, coho and chum salmon return to Noons Creek on their way to the hatchery. Harbour seals are often spotted in the inlet.

Boardwalk over the sedge marsh

For thousands of years, Coast Salish First Nations used the head of the inlet as a summer camp; middens and tools have been discovered throughout the area. History enthusiasts will enjoy a visit to the Port Moody Station Museum, adjacent to Rocky Point Park. As well as artifacts pertaining to the region, the museum offers an excellent leaflet entitled *Heritage Tour of Inlet Trail*.

> GETTING THERE From St. Johns Street (Highway 7A) in Port Moody, turn north on Moody Street. After crossing the railway on the overpass, follow the road around the curve, turn left on Murray Street and proceed to the parking area for Rocky Point Park on the left.

This starting point can be reached by public transit: Take the West Coast Express, or bus #160 from Vancouver, to Port Moody Station. Walk down Moody Street to Rocky Point Park. For up-to-date information, call TransLink at 604-953-3333 or visit their website at translink.ca.

> THE TRAIL Head for the waterfront to pick up Shoreline Trail and set off eastward. After crossing Slaughterhouse Creek, stay left on the pedestrian path as it enters a forest of firs and cedars with a rich

undergrowth of sword fern and salal. The last remnant of a wrecked fishing boat is visible from a small clearing.

Approaching the head of the inlet, you descend to a zigzag board-walk over tidal mudflats. Children will probably spot the decorative clay tiles set into the bridge posts. Take a short detour left to a viewing platform from where you look west along Burrard Inlet to the North Shore Mountains and, closer at hand, over a rich feeding ground for waterfowl, gulls and herons.

A short distance ahead is the mouth of Noons Creek. During October or November, the creek may be alive with salmon returning to spawn—and attendant predators. To visit Noons Creek Hatchery, take the trail to the right after the bridge, cross the cycle path and head upstream on the north side of the creek. In a few minutes you'll arrive at the hatchery building where, if volunteer staff is on hand, you may be able to see eggs at various stages in the incubating trays or salmon fry in the pond, depending on the season.

Returning to Shoreline Trail, your next diversion might be a side trip to the site of an old shingle mill, complete with the remains of a beehive burner. The bricks used in construction (you might have noticed some laid in the trail) were made at the Hutchinson brickyard, which prospered nearby until the 1940s. This foray is best made at low tide.

And so, continue through a final grove of poplars to Old Orchard Park, your turnaround point. A sandy beach and picnic tables invite you to linger before retracing your steps to Rocky Point. Be sure to walk to the end of the pier before returning to your car or transit.

BURNS POINT

Round trip 5 km (3 miles)
Allow 2 hours
Good all year

FAMILY HIKE
EASY

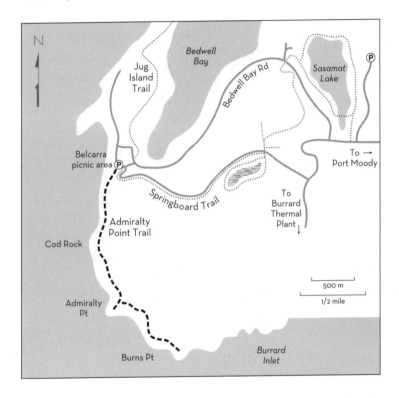

BELCARRA PICNIC AREA attracts crowds on summer weekends, as does White Pine Beach on nearby Sasamat Lake, but there is more to Belcarra Regional Park than these deservedly popular spots. As well as a short hike to Jug Island Beach (Hike 10) at the northern tip of the peninsula, the park's trail system has been extended to link Belcarra with Sasamat and Buntzen Lakes (see Hikes 11 and 13). Also, a cycling/walking path roughly parallels the aptly named

Wandering hemlock

Tum-tumay-whueton Drive—meaning "the biggest place for people"—from Bedwell Bay Road to the picnic area. The park leaflet
gives details of Belcarra's history as the site of two Salish villages;
middens dating back to 1200 BC have yielded shells, bones and broken stone tools.

Meanwhile, the shoreline walk to Burns Point is enjoyable in its
own right, with its succession of beaches and headlands and views
across Burrard Inlet. The trail is well marked, but here a word of

caution to the adventurous: Those tempting unmarked trails leading into the forest are part of a maze of old paths and tracks that defies description. Unless you know the area, stay on the designated trail.

> GETTING THERE From Highway 7A in Port Moody, turn north onto Ioco Road, staying on this road as it swings westward. Turn right on 1st Avenue, keep left on Bedwell Bay Road at the next fork and follow signs for Belcarra picnic area.

This starting point can be reached by public transit: Take the #C26 Belcarra bus from Port Moody Station and alight at Belcarra Bay Road and Midden Road, close to Belcarra picnic area. For up-to-date information, contact TransLink at 604-953-3333 or visit their website at translink.ca.

> THE TRAIL The trail to Admiralty and Burns Points, signposted Admiralty Point Trail, heads into the forest from behind the washroom building at the south end of the main parking lot. Or you can take Springboard Trail from in front of the washrooms and go right on Admiralty Point Trail.

After crossing a road leading to private property, you tread the soft path beneath the trees. Here and there, reminders of long-gone squatters' homes can be seen in the patches of periwinkle and other garden flowers still bravely occupying the little clearings.

About a half mile from the start, Cod Rock, off to the right, provides an open view across the inlet. Your next port of call, Maple Beach, is a sheltered spot beside the water. A few minutes after leaving the beach you will come to a fork, the right-hand path being a side trail to Admiralty Point—a good place for spotting seals as well as admiring the more obvious views of Mount Seymour and the Ironworkers Memorial (Second Narrows) Bridge.

Returning to the main trail, you continue to Whiteshell Bank, after which you must climb quite steeply before descending to the open bluff above Burns Point—regrettably the end of the trail but a fine place to picnic, with the tugboats and other river traffic passing by below.

10

JUG ISLAND BEACH

**Belcarra Regional Park
Port Moody**

Round trip 5.5 km (3½ miles)
Allow 2½ hours

Good all year

EASY

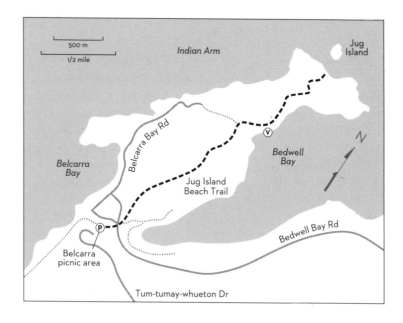

THIS DOUGHTY LITTLE hike from Belcarra picnic area to a tucked-away beach at the tip of the Bedwell Bay peninsula will please hikers looking for some ups and downs and not deterred by the occasional rocky pitch. The second-growth forest of hemlocks and broad-leafed maples is cool and shady on a warm day and brilliant in fall, when gold and crimson leaves carpet the ground. The pebbly beach at trail's end invites exploration and provides a view across Indian Arm to Woodlands and Mount Seymour. The granite dome offshore is, of course, Jug Island. The rock once had a "handle," hence its name, but this has long since eroded away.

> **GETTING THERE** From Highway 7A in Port Moody, turn north onto Ioco Road, staying on this road as it swings westward. Turn right on 1st Avenue, keep left on Bedwell Bay Road at the next fork and follow signs for Belcarra picnic area.

This starting point can be reached by public transit: Take the #C26 Belcarra bus from Port Moody Station and alight at Belcarra Bay Road and Midden Road, close to Belcarra picnic area. For up-to-date information, contact TransLink at 604-953-3333 or visit their website at translink.ca.

> **THE TRAIL** Walk between the covered picnic shelters to spot the sign to Jug Island Beach. Follow the path through the woods, cross the road and take Jug Island Trail to the left. After a gradual ascent, the wide gravel trail (once an old logging road) levels off and eventually skirts a looming rock wall clothed with mosses. Ahead is a wooden staircase, beyond which the trail continues to rise and descend along the ridge. Whilst watching your step over the rocks, you might notice that in places the granite underfoot is scored or furrowed from over-riding glaciers eons ago.

After passing a hydro right-of-way on your left (there's a Jug Island sign at this point), you climb to an east-facing viewpoint overlooking Bedwell Bay and the hillside opposite. A short distance beyond this high point, you begin the steep descent to the beach. Driftwood offers a seat for lunch or a rest, while you watch cormorants, loons and goldeneyes bobbing and diving in the water. Harbour seals, too, can often be spotted from this secluded cove.

Your return to Belcarra is by the same route, though you could opt for a more civilized variation by taking the hydro right-of-way passed earlier. This track soon brings you to a yellow gate onto a dead-end road. Follow this to Belcarra Bay Road and walk back to the park past the fine residences perched on the cliffs overlooking the bay.

11

Belcarra Regional Park
Port Moody

WOODHAVEN-
SASAMAT TRAILS

Round trip 7 km (4½ miles)
Allow 3 hours
Good all year

FAMILY HIKE

EASY

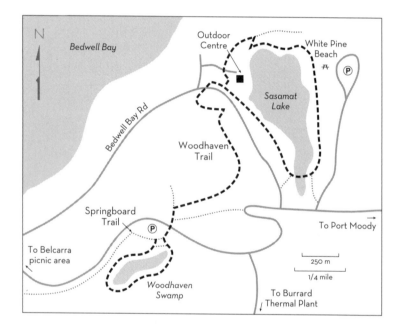

N

Bedwell Bay

Outdoor
Centre

White Pine
Beach

P

Sasamat
Lake

Bedwell Bay Rd

Woodhaven
Trail

Springboard
Trail

P

To Port Moody

To Belcarra
picnic area

250 m

1/4 mile

Woodhaven
Swamp

To Burrard
Thermal Plant

THIS VARIED LOW-LEVEL hike links two dissimilar bodies of water within Belcarra Regional Park. Using the Woodhaven Gate parking lot as a starting point, you can take an unusual walk around a swamp before descending through the forest to circumnavigate and enjoy the amenities of Sasamat Lake. If you prefer solitude on your outing, best to make this an out-of-season walk—Sasamat Lake is enormously popular on fine summer weekends.

Skunk cabbage

> **GETTING THERE** From Highway 7A in Port Moody, turn north onto Ioco Road, staying on this road as it swings westward. Turn right on 1st Avenue, keep left on Bedwell Bay Road at the next fork and follow signs for Belcarra picnic area. The Woodhaven Gate parking lot is on the left about 2.5 km (1½ miles) from the beginning of the park drive.

Although this starting point cannot be reached by public transit, you could (in summer only) take the #C26 Belcarra bus from Port Moody Station to White Pine Beach at Sasamat Lake and join the hiking route at midpoint. For up-to-date information, contact Trans-Link at 604-953-3333 or visit their website at translink.ca.

> **THE TRAIL** Below the parking area, look for the Woodhaven Swamp Loop Trail and begin a counter-clockwise circuit. Views of the drowned forest open out as you walk along the edge of the swamp, skunk cabbage and yellow pond lilies brightening the eerie scene; less noticeable are insect-eating sundew plants colonizing fallen logs. After passing through stands of large evergreens, you will reach a viewing platform. A few metres beyond the end of the

boardwalk, an informal path on the right leads you to the multi-use Springboard Trail to begin the next stage of your journey.

Walk downhill for a short distance to where a service road joins on the left. Take this, passing the continuation of the multi-use trail on your right (an optional return route), until you come to the sign-posted hikers' trail to Sasamat Lake. On this you meander through semi-open forest, over bumps and into hollows, the descent gradually becoming steeper until flights of stairs ease your way past some houses and onto Bedwell Bay Road.

Pick up the trail across the road and follow Windermere Creek upstream to a bridge. Go left over the bridge and climb the path and steps up to a road leading to Sasamat Outdoor Centre. Cross the road and continue along the track beyond the yellow gate. After a short distance, descend the wooden staircase on your right and follow Sasamat Lake Loop Trail to White Pine Beach. Here, on a winter's day or in less-than-perfect weather, you may enjoy a lunch spot beneath the pines, with only birds and squirrels for company.

Follow the footpath to continue, but at the second beach area, walk across the sand to stay with the lakeshore trail. After crossing the floating walkway at the marshy end of the lake, you have a choice. You can continue along the Sasamat Lake Loop Trail to Windermere Creek Bridge and from there retrace your steps, returning well exercised to Woodhaven Gate. If you opt for a shorter route to your car, climb the left-hand trail to Bedwell Bay Road, walk left for about 250 m (275 yards), then right on the access road to Belcarra picnic area. At the first bend, pick up the multi-use Springboard Trail as it enters the woods through the yellow barrier, thereafter climbing gently to the service road from which you set out on Woodhaven Trail.

12

BUNTZEN RIDGE

**Belcarra Regional Park
Port Moody/Anmore**

Round trip 6 km (3³⁄4 miles)
High point 350 m (1150 feet)
Elevation gain 290 m (950 feet)

Allow 2¹⁄2 hours
Best March to November
MODERATELY EASY

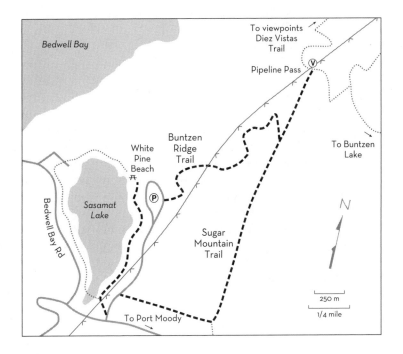

THANKS TO A trail linking Sasamat Lake in Belcarra Regional
Park to Buntzen Lake, an interesting circular outing can be made,
with the pass between the two lakes as a possible destination. Easy
hikers not averse to some climbing will enjoy the idyllic forest trail
and views from Pipeline Pass, before returning via Sugar Mountain Trail and the shore of Sasamat Lake to the White Pine picnic
grounds and swimming beach.

> GETTING THERE To reach Sasamat Lake from Highway 7A in
Port Moody, turn north onto Ioco Road. Follow this road as it swings
westward, and turn right on 1st Avenue. At the next fork, go left on
Bedwell Bay Road and right at the turnoff to White Pine Beach.

This starting point can be reached by public transit in summer
only, when the Belcarra bus #C26 from Port Moody Station goes to
White Pine Beach. For up-to-date information, contact TransLink at
604-953-3333 or visit their website at translink.ca.

> THE TRAIL Saving the lakeshore for your return, begin by search-
ing out Buntzen Ridge Trail—easiest found by making your way to
the northeast end of the upper arm of the vehicle loop, where a signpost sets you on your way.

After about 10 minutes of climbing, the trail crosses a powerline
right-of-way, thereafter zigzagging steeply upward through second-
growth forest of tall, straight trees and glades of sword fern to a junction with the equestrian Sugar Mountain Trail—your return route.
Turn left, pressing on toward the ridge, until you meet the Diez Vistas Trail from Buntzen Lake and break out into the open in Pipeline Pass. Here you could scramble up to a lofty perch on the north
side of the powerline for a lunch spot with a partial view of Buntzen
Lake. Or, if a further 30 minutes and 150 m (500 feet) of climbing
does not deter you, go past the disused water pipe and follow Diez
Vistas Trail to the first of its viewpoints, a west-facing bluff with a
grand view over Sasamat Lake, Bedwell Bay and Indian Arm. Resist
the temptation to ramble far along Diez Vistas Trail—it is a six-hour
hike at the end of which you would need to climb back to Pipeline
Pass from Buntzen Lake.

To complete your Sasamat–Buntzen Ridge circuit, simply stay
on Sugar Mountain Trail as it descends gently to a powerline before
plunging more steeply westward to a gate on the White Pine access
road. From there, walk a few metres toward Bedwell Bay Road to
pick up a trail marked "Beach," on which you quickly join the Sasamat Lake Loop Trail at the east end of a floating walkway. A relaxing 15-minute walk along the lakeshore takes you back to White
Pine Beach.

13

BUNTZEN LAKE CIRCUIT

Round trip 10 km (6 miles)
High point 230 m (750 feet)
Elevation gain 75 m (250 feet)
Allow 4½ hours

Good all year
FAMILY HIKE
MODERATELY EASY

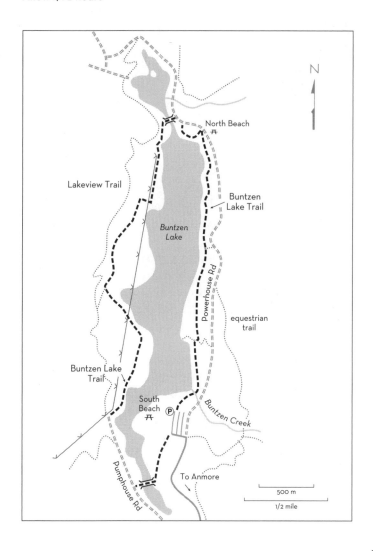

Buntzen Lake

THIS LOW-LEVEL CIRCUIT around the 5-km- (3-mile-) long
Buntzen Lake reservoir makes a satisfying hike for all seasons. It is
not too much for an active family, and it offers beautiful picnic sites
at both south and north beaches.

> GETTING THERE From Highway 7A in Port Moody, turn north
onto Ioco Road, staying on this road as it swings westward. Turn
right on 1st Avenue, go right at the next fork and follow Sunnyside
Road through Anmore to the entrance to Buntzen Lake recreation
area. Drive the access road for 2 km (1¼ miles) to the third parking
bay at South Beach.

This starting point can be reached by public transit on summer
weekends and holidays only, when the Belcarra bus #C26 from Port
Moody Station goes to South Beach. For up-to-date information, contact TransLink at 604-953-3333 or visit their website at translink.ca.

> THE TRAIL As the trails on the lake's west side are the most
demanding, we suggest a clockwise circuit. The Buntzen Lake
Trail—your route for the entire hike—is picked up at the southwest
corner of the parking lot, beyond the warden's office.

After a short stretch of forest, you cross the marshy end of the lake on a long floating bridge. Now begins your northward journey. Where the gravel road ends, take the right fork, staying with the marked hikers' trail thereafter as it winds through woods notable for their abundance and variety of mosses and fungi.

You will emerge eventually onto a powerline (which you crossed earlier), and views now unfold of the lake and Eagle Ridge opposite. A bluff on the powerline right-of-way might be a good lunch spot, or you can set your sights on the picnic tables at North Beach, visible across the water.

Shortly after the trail reaches lake level, a sign "To Powerhouse Rd." directs you right to a bridge across the narrow neck of the lake and North Beach. This fine bridge, built in 1991 by the Canadian Forces, Chilliwack, saves a 30-minute tramp along the service road around the lake's northern tip.

You can leave the beach from its southern end, near the outfall of the submountain tunnel. Climb the steps to pick up Buntzen Lake Trail for its final 3 km (2 miles) along the east side of the lake. This is a delightful stretch of trail, on which you occasionally descend to the water's edge and cross several creeks before arriving back at South Beach—and your welcome transport.

COLONY FARM—
RIVERVIEW LANDS

Round trip 9.6 km (6 miles)   Good all year
Allow 3 hours   **EASY**

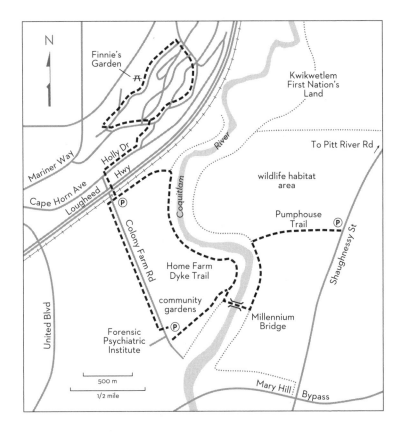

THE OLD FARMLAND on both sides of the Coquitlam River near its confluence with the Fraser River was once managed and worked by patients of Riverview Hospital. After the farm's closure in 1985, the land was saved from development by the efforts of Burke

Millennium Bridge

Mountain Naturalists and other community organizations. Today, the lands are a prime bird-watching site, with well-kept dyke paths enjoyed by walkers, joggers and cyclists. Community garden plots occupy a corner of the green oasis.

Described here is a walk combining Colony Farm with Riverview Lands, the site of western Canada's first arboretum. From European lindens to a dawn redwood from China, the magnificent collection of trees from around the world graces the lawns. To learn more about the arboretum or to join a guided walking tour, contact Riverview Horticultural Centre Society at 604-299-9910 or visit their website at rhcs.org. A fitting destination for this doubly interesting walk is Finnie's Garden, created in 1951 by nurse Art Finnie and patients of Riverview as a horticultural therapy project. Today, the Horticultural Society helps with the upkeep of the garden.

> GETTING THERE The walk starts from a roadside parking area on Shaughnessy Street in Port Coquitlam. This trailhead is reached by driving north on Shaughnessy Street from the Mary Hill Bypass for

about 1 km (½ mile) or south on Shaughnessy Street from Pitt River Road for a little more than 2 km (1¼ miles).

This starting point is accessible by public transit: Take the #159 bus from Port Coquitlam Station, alight at Citadel Drive and Shaughnessy Street and walk to the starting point. For up-to-date information, contact TransLink at 604-953-3333 or visit their website at translink.ca.

> THE TRAIL Descending to Pumphouse Trail, you find yourself beside a marsh or a lake, depending on the season. In winter, you might see mergansers and teal among the resident mallards and perhaps a lone coyote loping across the old field habitat. Turn left when you reach the Coquitlam River dyke and set your sights on the arched Millennium Bridge. From its deck you have a close view of the river and a wide view of Colony Farm lands and the mountains around Pitt Lake.

Cross the bridge and set off northward on the dyke path, a ditch on your left and the river on your right behind a fringe of bushes. In spring, watch for hummingbirds around the salmonberry flowers; later, various warblers arrive and cedar waxwings come to feed on red elderberries. When you come to a trail junction, you must go left, Sheep Paddocks Trail ahead being closed for repairs until further notice. Follow the left-hand path (Mundy Creek Trail) to Colony Farm Road.

Cross the railway, then cross Lougheed Highway at the traffic lights. From Cape Horn Avenue turn right on Holly Drive to enter Riverview Lands. Stay left on Holly Drive at the junction with Pine Terrace, turn left and uphill at the next junction (you are now on Fern Terrace) and stay left again on Fern Terrace until you reach a sign for Violet Way. Join Violet Way for a few metres, then go right on Kerria Drive beyond the vehicle barrier. Keep right where the road forks, and, after passing some buildings, you'll come to Finnie's Garden. Picnic tables invite you to rest and eat, but take time afterwards to visit the fish pond and explore the paths and stone terraces. Don't miss the Horticultural Society's shed with its mural of plants that grow in the garden.

Leaving the garden, continue along Kerria Drive, turn right at the T-junction and walk down Oak Crescent until you reach Holly

Drive. A right turn here will take you back to Cape Horn Avenue, ready to re-cross the Lougheed Highway. Now follow the path along the west side of Colony Farm Road. If you're so inclined, stroll among the community garden plots before making for the southeast corner of the parking area to find Garden Trail heading northward beside a ditch. At its end, climb up to the dyke path from a small bridge, backtrack a few steps to cross the Millennium Bridge, and you're set to retrace your outward route via Pumphouse Trail to Shaughnessy Street.

BURKE MOUNTAIN WOODLAND TRAIL

Round trip 7 km (4¹/₂ miles)
High point 500 m (1640 feet)
Elevation gain 200 m
(650 feet)

Allow 3¹/₂ hours
Best April to November
MODERATELY EASY

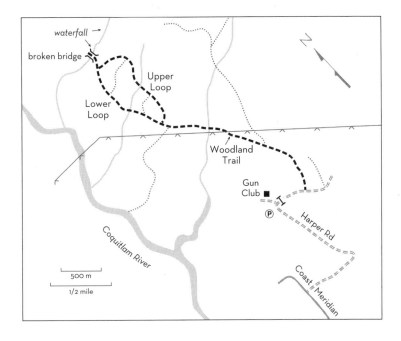

THIS SHORT HIKE on the lower slope of Burke Mountain is one
of several marked out and maintained by the Burke Mountain Naturalists as part of their efforts to promote the preservation of the Burke
Mountain/Pinecone Lake wilderness area as a park. The route uses
old logging roads and forest paths to reach its end at a breathtaking waterfall. Be sure to include the Upper Loop Trail: it is impossible not to catch the spirit of the long-gone majestic forest as you

Coltsfoot

walk the old skid roads among the stumps and shells of giant cedars. Other relics of logging days are there for you to discover.

> GETTING THERE To reach the start of the hike from Highway 7 in Coquitlam, drive north on Coast Meridian for about 5 km (3 miles). Turn right onto Harper Road and drive as far as the gun club sign. Park near the yellow gate.

> THE TRAIL Begin by going through the gate and up the gravel road, heading left after about 10 minutes onto an old road. At the next fork, signed "Woodland Walk," keep left again. In spring, this stretch is lined with brilliant mosses, yellow violets and coltsfoot. You will cross a creek at a waterfall before breaking into the open alongside a powerline. This soon opens out further into a clearing with a view westward toward Eagle Ridge across the Coquitlam River Valley.

Woodland Trail now heads northward from the clearing. After following markers to detour around a collapsed bridge, take the Upper Loop Trail entering the woods on the right. Be careful now to follow the blue markers and stay with the Upper Loop as it gains height and meanders through the forest, crossing several creeks along the way. Eventually, coming to a sign directing you to the falls, you descend to rejoin the Lower Loop Trail. Turn right here to proceed to the trail's end, passing on your way a cedar stump of awe-inspiring dimensions.

The trail ends abruptly at an old broken bridge spanning a narrow gorge. From the steep little path below a giant Douglas-fir you can view the waterfall, a thrilling sight at spring run-off, as the water tumbles through the forested canyon.

You can return to the powerline by staying on the Lower Loop Trail. Ignore trails joining from the left, but follow the markers again to avoid the collapsed bridge. From the clearing, retrace your steps to the yellow gate near the gun club.

DE BOVILLE SLOUGH

Round trip 9.2 km (5¾ miles)   Good all year
Allow 3 hours or more   **EASY**

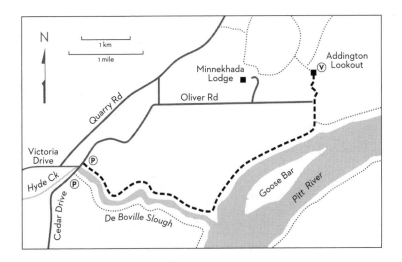

FOR NATURE LOVERS, this is a journey into Arcadia. Birds and animals love these waterways; flowering plants and shrubs thrive around the dykes and ditches. Every season has its bounty: Spring brings swallows and warblers to the area; in September, chum salmon head up the slough to spawn in Hyde Creek; fall sees an influx of wintering hawks and bald eagles and, as the weather turns colder, large numbers of waterfowl move into the sheltered ditches. Take binoculars, for sure.

Burke Mountain Naturalists produce excellent free brochures for this region. You can visit their website at bmn.ca or write to them at P.O. Box 52540, RPO Coquitlam Centre, Coquitlam, B.C., V3B 7J4.

De Boville Slough and the Pitt River dyke can be linked with trails in Minnekhada Regional Park (Hike 17) for a longer hike, though many will be content with Addington Lookout for a destination and turnaround point, as described here.

Basking turtles

> **GETTING THERE** From Highway 7 (Lougheed Highway) in Port Coquitlam, drive north on Coast Meridian Road. In slightly more than 1 km (½ mile) turn right (east) on Prairie Road. Turn left on Cedar Drive and follow this to its junction with Lower Victoria Drive at De Boville Slough gate. There are parking lots both south and north of the slough.

This starting point can be reached by public transit: Take the West Coast Express, or bus #160 from Vancouver, to Port Coquitlam Station and bus #C38 to Victoria Drive and Cedar Drive. For up-to-date information, contact TransLink at 604-953-3333 or visit their website at translink.ca.

> **THE TRAIL** Set off along the north-side dyke, pausing to read about wetland habitat at the information kiosk. Walking eastward toward the Pitt River, you have mountain views ahead, blueberry fields inland. The ditch on your left is frequented by mallards, wood ducks, gadwalls and hooded mergansers. Among the tangled shrubs and grasses between the dyke and the slough, you might be lucky enough to spot the small, green-backed heron—a not-so-common resident of the area.

Arriving at the confluence of the slough and the Pitt River, you follow the dyke path upstream and the scene changes. River tugs work among the log booms while grebes swim and dive in the fast-flowing current and cormorants dry their wings atop the pilings. In spring, you might see black-tailed deer browsing at the edges of the inland fields or coyotes loping among the rows of blueberry bushes. Later in the year, don't be surprised to see a black bear or two feasting on ripe berries.

As you approach Addington Marsh and the caretaker's residence, head left (north) on the long straight dyke. Minnekhada's High Knoll looms ahead. Continue past the end of Oliver Road and gird yourself for a short scramble to Addington Lookout. Here you may rest or picnic on the platform or on the rocks below, with a grand view of the marsh and polder and the mountains of the UBC Malcolm Knapp Research Forest (Hike 47) beyond. Less picturesque is the Sheridan Hill quarry opposite; when they shut down for lunch around noon, you will be able to hear birdsong again.

As you retrace your steps to Cedar Drive, there will be other things to see—a ring-necked pheasant perhaps or a circling osprey or turtles sunning themselves on logs in the ditch, their necks and legs stretched fore and aft. There is always something new to discover when you pass by a second time.

MINNEKHADA

Round trip 6.5 km (4 miles)   Good all year
High point 180 m (600 feet)   FAMILY HIKE
Elevation gain 150 m (500 feet)   **EASY**
Allow 3 hours

COQUITLAM'S MINNEKHADA Regional Park is a joy for walkers throughout the year. A network of signposted trails crosses and encircles the 219 ha (542 acres) of marsh and lowland forest. There are several viewpoints overlooking the marsh, Addington Point and the Pitt River. Details of Minnekhada's historical background and

Crossing Log Walk bridge

other facilities for visitors can be found on the notice board in the parking lot. Also available are trail maps to complete the picture presented here and invite further exploration.

The route suggested gives a sampling of forest, marsh and knoll, easily accomplished by an active family in a half day. As well as waterfowl, herons and hawks, the area is much frequented by songbirds. By late May, every nest box harbours a family of swallows, and the marsh resounds with the musical twanging of bullfrogs. Take binoculars.

> **GETTING THERE** From Highway 7 (Lougheed Highway) in Coquitlam, turn left (north) onto Coast Meridian (staying left to avoid the overpass). In 2.5 km (1½ miles) turn left on Victoria Drive. After a further kilometre, take the left turn on the crest of the hill to continue on Victoria Drive. It is 3.5 km (2 miles) from this turning to the parking area on Quarry Road.

> **THE TRAIL** Soon after leaving the parking lot, go right on Lodge Trail. When you see the glint of water through the trees, stay right and soon you'll emerge beside the lower marsh. After crossing the

outlet creek, your route takes you past a picnic site below the access road to Minnekhada Lodge before continuing in an easterly direction through the forest on Fern Trail.

About 800 m (½ mile) from the picnic area, you'll arrive at a trail junction. The path to the right leads to Addington Lookout (see De Boville Slough, Hike 16). This fairly steep 20-minute side trip offers a panoramic view of Addington Marsh, a 400-ha (900-acre) refuge for fish and waterfowl. Beyond, you see the Pitt Polder Ecological Reserve, backed by Golden Ears.

Retracing your steps to the junction with Fern Trail (loop trails are currently in poor condition), continue uphill around the base of a high cliff. In less than 400 m (¼ mile), you'll see a trail on your left signposted to Low Knoll. The five-minute side trip to this rocky outcrop overlooking the lower marsh is worth the effort. Returning to the main trail, stay right at the next fork (Mid-marsh Trail is your return route) and continue for a further 5 to 10 minutes until you come to a signposted path on your right leading to High Knoll— your destination and turnaround point. This rocky bluff, attained after a short, stiff climb, is the highest point in the park. As you eat your lunch under the watchful eyes of hawks and eagles, you can look out to the south and west and observe the marsh below.

When it is time to leave, retrace your steps to the junction signposted to Mid-marsh Trail, and go right. After negotiating a scramble and some minor bluffs you will descend to marsh level at a dyke. Flocks of geese and ducks can usually be seen on the body of water on your right.

The path going straight ahead from the bridge at the west end of the dyke, Log Walk, will take you back toward Quarry Road. Turn left (south) when you meet Quarry Trail, staying right at subsequent junctions to find your car.

CAPILANO CANYON

Round trip 9 km (5½ miles)   Good all year
Allow 3½ hours   **EASY**

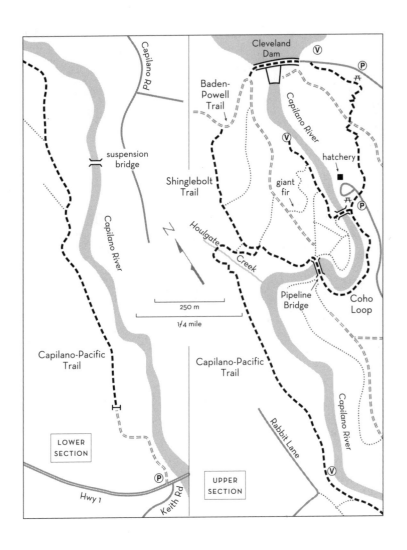

Capilano Lake

AS WELL AS visiting the Capilano fish hatchery and the Cleveland Dam, this hike explores several miles of the forested Capilano Canyon along park trails named to commemorate the region's logging history. Who could resist following the route of a shinglebolt flume laid by the Burrard Inlet Flume & Boom Company in 1909?

> GETTING THERE Leave Highway 1/99 (Upper Levels Highway) in West Vancouver at exit 13 and drive south on Taylor Way. Turn left (east) onto Keith Road. Continue for 1.6 km (1 mile) to where the pavement ends, under the bridge. Park here.

This starting point may be accessible by public transit: Bus #256 from Park Royal uses Spuraway Lodge as its turnaround point, from where you could walk to the end of Keith Road and the parking area. For up-to-date information, contact TransLink at 604-953-3333 or visit their website at translink.ca.

> THE TRAIL Walk along the powerline right-of-way (formerly an old logging railway grade) north from the gravel parking area. About 1 km (½ mile) beyond the yellow posts, follow the signposted Capilano-Pacific Trail into the woods.

Walking beneath stately hemlocks and cedars, you soon arrive at an observation platform that offers a dramatic view of the canyon.

After a further 10 minutes of walking, a series of stairs and bridges lead you to a crossing of Houlgate Creek. Ignore a trail rising steeply to your left and continue to a trail junction with a map and signpost. Turn right here onto Upper Shinglebolt Trail. On this you descend, staying right when you reach the gravel road, to cross Capilano River on the Pipeline Bridge.

On the east bank, turn left on Coho Loop (now part of the Trans Canada Trail) and continue upstream past Dog Leg Pool to a small suspension bridge near the picnic area. For a 15-minute side trip to the viewing decks at Second Canyon, cross the bridge and walk upstream. From the safety of the platforms you can gaze upward to the spillway of the Cleveland Dam. Returning, you could take a further diversion to visit the canyon's largest old-growth Douglas-fir.

To resume your circuit, return to the hatchery and look for the trail to the Cleveland Dam (named Palisades on the park map) ascending from the roadway turnaround near a whimsical wooden toadstool. After a short, steep climb, the trail crosses a gravel service road and carries on up several flights of stairs to emerge in the picnic grounds below the parking lot.

The return trip begins on the west side of the dam. Leaving the cleared area, take the right-hand fork of the gravel road, signed Baden-Powell Trail. Watch now for Shinglebolt Trail heading left into the woods. On this you descend gently through open forest, staying right where the trail forks, to a fenced clearing, from which you descend more steeply via several staircases, to step out onto an old skid road. Walk left for a few metres then take the trail branching right (there's a red metal marker) up a rooty bank, from the top of which you descend wooden steps to continue southward on Shinglebolt Trail. When you reach the familiar junction with Capilano-Pacific, turn right to re-cross Houlgate Creek and retrace your steps homeward, having explored much of the Capilano River's rugged canyon.

LOWER GROUSE CIRCUIT

Round trip 8 km (5 miles)   **Allow** 4 hours
High point 500 m (1640 feet)   Best April to November
Elevation gain 350 m   **MODERATELY DIFFICULT**
(1150 feet)

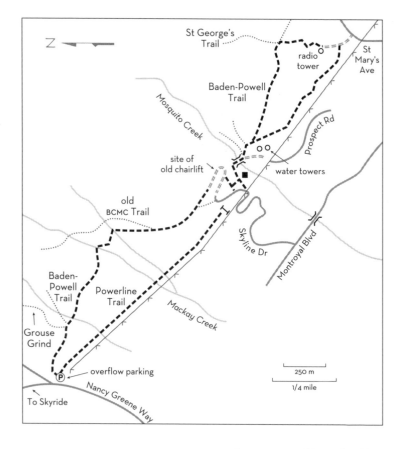

ALL-SEASON HIKERS HAVE good reason to bless the Boy Scouts for the many miles of their Baden-Powell Trail at lower elevations. Walkers undaunted by some rough, steep sections can

Mackay Creek

tackle the entire route described. A midway connection at Skyline Drive makes easier variations possible.

> **GETTING THERE** Drive north on Capilano Road and Nancy Greene Way in North Vancouver to the Grouse Mountain Skyride. Park in the overflow (Grouse Grind) parking lot on the east side of the road.

This starting point can be reached by public transit: Take the Grouse Mountain bus #236 from Lonsdale Quay SeaBus Terminal to Grouse Mountain Skyride. For up-to-date information, contact TransLink at 604-953-3333 or visit their website at translink.ca.

> **THE TRAIL** You will spot the joint Grouse Grind and Baden-Powell trailhead above the parking lot. Please note that the Grouse Grind is likely to be closed during the winter months, preventing access to the Baden-Powell here. In this case, go through the gate onto the powerline and take a trail heading sharply uphill from just beyond the second wooden power pole. In a few minutes you will join the Baden-Powell, turning right to continue your journey. Or, for an easier hike, you could stay on the powerline right-of-way to Skyline Drive and, using the map, pick up the Baden-Powell at Mosquito Creek.

Let's assume you pass unhindered through the wire gate at the joint trailhead. A short distance along the well-used trail, where Grinders head left, you follow the Baden-Powell markers straight ahead for your more interesting trek across the lower slopes of Grouse Mountain. After about 40 minutes of climbing, during which you ignore side trails and concentrate on the rocks and roots underfoot, the gradient eases. Next, you must cross two branches of Mackay Creek, the second a debris-choked ravine caused by severe flooding some years ago. Although a simple bridge spans the creek, some scrambling may be necessary in this area.

Descending at last, ignore both the old BCMC Trail branching uphill and a shortcut descending to Skyline Drive and follow Baden-Powell signs through what was once the parking lot for an old chairlift, down a steep bank to the Mosquito Creek Bridge. When you are ready to leave the pools and boulders, follow the trail markers around the water towers to resume your eastward journey through the forest. At a confusing trail junction, keep straight ahead toward Mountain Highway.

About a half hour after leaving the creek, you'll reach a viewpoint with a bench at the junction with St. George's Trail. Go downhill to the right here, join the service road and turn right again when you reach the powerline. Now you are set for the homeward journey. Continue west along the right-of-way for about 15 minutes until a signpost directs you into the forest to rejoin the Baden-Powell for the re-crossing of Mosquito Creek.

After climbing up the west side of the creek, you will need to apply your navigational skills once more to get yourself back to the powerline. Instead of climbing the steep bank that leads to the old chairlift parking lot, go straight ahead, past the house with the orange roof. Skirting another residence, go downhill on Skyline Drive to the next bend, where a gated track leads to the powerline right-of-way.

The final 2 km (1¼ miles) of mostly level walking take you through the catchment area for unruly Mackay Creek before returning you to the Skyride, having accomplished a respectable 8-km (5-mile) hike.

OLD LILLOOET TRAIL

Round trip 10 km (6 miles)   Good all year
Allow 3½ hours   **MODERATELY EASY**

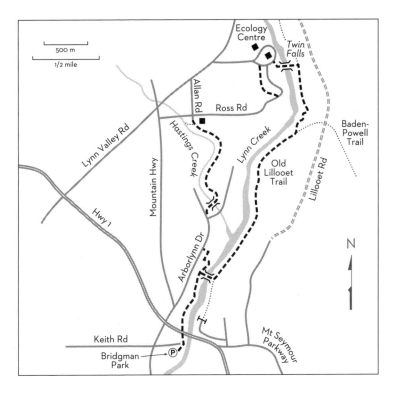

THIS SURPRISINGLY ENERGETIC circuit in the lower Lynn Creek valley is named after an old cattle trail from the Interior to Burrard Inlet. To reach this remnant of B.C. history, however, you must first pass under two highways and skirt a landfill site. Thereafter, your surroundings abruptly change to semi-wilderness as you work your way upstream to your turnaround point in Lynn Canyon Park. The route is accessible throughout the year, but beware of slippery steps and bridges in wet or frosty weather.

Picnic area, Lynn Canyon

> **GETTING THERE** The best starting point for this outing is Bridgman Park on Keith Road East. Driving north from the Ironworkers Memorial (Second Narrows) Bridge, leave Highway 1 at exit 21, turn left on Mountain Highway and left again on Keith Road, watching for the entrance to Bridgman Park on your right.

This starting point may be accessible by public transit. Several buses from Phibbs Exchange go to the intersection of Mountain Highway and Keith Road East, from where you could walk to Bridgman Park. For up-to-date information, contact TransLink at 604-953-3333 or visit their website at translink.ca.

> **THE TRAIL** From the east side of the parking lot, the trail heads north to take you safely beneath the Keith Road and Highway 1 bridges, after which you proceed more peacefully along the west bank of Lynn Creek. After about 10 minutes of walking, you'll come to a footbridge spanning the creek; cross to the east side and continue upstream on the civilized pathway.

In less than 1.6 km (1 mile) you will reach the start of the (unmarked) Old Lillooet Trail, just beyond the sign for Morten Creek. Urban evidence is left behind as you follow the red metal markers up through the forest. After a section of boardwalks, you must pick your way among rocks and roots as you climb high above the creek.

Eventually the trail levels off before meeting the Baden-Powell Trail, at which point you stay left on an unmarked trail to descend sharply to creek level. After a long boardwalk beside a beach, the trail follows the creek upstream until it reaches the wooden bridge at Twin Falls in Lynn Canyon Park. After crossing the bridge and surmounting the two long staircases to the canyon's rim, head right (north) on the gravel track and in a few minutes you will arrive in front of the Lynn Canyon Park building, with its café and other facilities. A spacious picnic area lies behind it. The Lynn Canyon Ecology Centre, near the suspension bridge, has imaginative displays and a wealth of information on the social and natural history of the Lynn Valley.

To begin the homeward leg of your circuit, return to the lower picnic area behind the café and walk up the road on the south side of the picnic grounds. Just before you reach the stop sign at the beginning of the loop road, look for a trail heading left into the woods; three large rocks mark its beginning. Keep left where a path heads right toward residences. Your trail parallels the park drive for about a half mile before emerging onto it at a bend. (You could, of course, have reached this point by walking down the park drive itself, following the sign for Ross Road Trail.)

Prepare yourself now for a 10-minute tramp along the park drive and Ross Road until you come to Allan Road. Turn left here. At road's end, by the schoolyard, walk straight ahead along the back of the playing fields to find the trail leading down the stairs into Hastings Creek Park. Stay left at the foot of the stairs to follow the creek downstream on its east side. The rough trail, with its many steps, accompanies Hastings Creek for almost 1.6 km (1 mile) to end at a bridge on the other side of which a wide track leads to the junction of Hoskins Road and Arborlynn Drive. Your route is south along Arborlynn for a short distance to where, just past Birchlynn Place, a well-marked trail descends into the woods on the left. Soon you are beside Lynn Creek once again, this time heading for home along its west bank. Retrace your steps through the highway underpasses to return to Bridgman Park.

LYNN HEADWATERS

Round trip 10 km (6 miles) **Allow** 3½ hours
High point 350 m (1150 feet) Best May to November
Elevation gain 150 m (500 feet) **MODERATELY EASY**

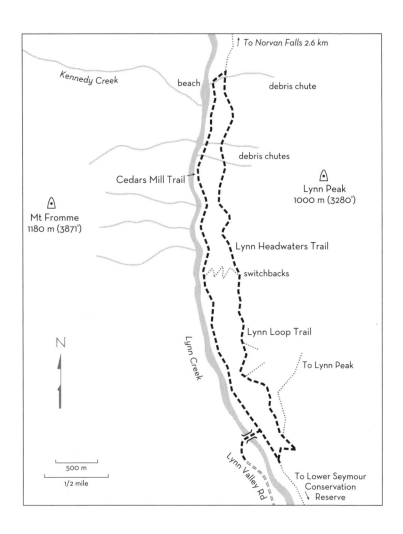

Trillium

IN 1981, when storms damaged the intakes, Lynn watershed was abandoned as the source of North Vancouver's water supply; in 1985, Lynn Headwaters Regional Park came into being. This extensive wilderness area, logged in the 1800s, is now accessible to hikers. The low-level trails offer excellent hiking from May onwards.

> GETTING THERE Leave Highway 1/99 (Upper Levels Highway) at exit 19 and drive north on Lynn Valley Road. Stay straight ahead where Dempsey Road branches left and continue to the park entrance.

> THE TRAIL After crossing to the east side of Lynn Creek at the dam beside the old water intakes, you will come to a notice board with a map and registration forms for hikers. We suggest a counterclockwise circuit incorporating Lynn Loop, Lynn Headwaters and Cedars Mill Trails.

Begin by walking downstream (south) on the gravel road to a signpost where Lynn Loop Trail leaves the road and plunges left into the forest. Edged by salal and Oregon grape, this excellent trail along the benchland of the Lynn Valley was made by the Federation of Mountain Clubs of B.C.

After you pass the trail to Lynn Peak striking off to the right, followed by a side trail to a viewpoint, an easy gradient is maintained as you walk on through the forest of tall hemlocks and cedars and the 100-year-old stumps of their predecessors. Mount Fromme can be glimpsed across the valley.

An hour's walking from the start brings you to a junction, from which Lynn Loop Trail descends steeply to Lynn Creek. Your benchland path now becomes Lynn Headwaters Trail and on it you continue for a further 2.5 km (1½ miles), taking in your stride some rougher terrain and many bridges.

Eventually, you arrive at a signposted junction—your turnaround point. From here, Headwaters Trail continues for 2.6 km (1½ miles) to Norvan Falls, where it connects with the Hanes Valley route to Grouse Mountain—a challenging hike best left to experts. Pick your way across the rocky slope to your left to a cleared area beside Lynn Creek. Logs offer a good lunch spot with a fine view upstream and across the valley toward Kennedy Creek.

Homeward bound, the riverside trail takes you through a grove of birches, then into evergreens, as you approach the site of Cedars Mill. You will realize from the rusty artifacts propped against trees and hanging from branches that you are walking through a casual logging museum. Also interesting are several bear-clawed tree trunks in the vicinity.

Soon after leaving the mill site, you will find yourself rejoining Lynn Loop Trail at the foot of the connector. The final leg of the circuit is an easy walk southward, mainly on an old road alongside the dashing, green waters of Lynn Creek.

LOWER SEYMOUR CONSERVATION RESERVE

Round trip 10 km (6 miles)
Allow 3½ hours
Good most of the year

FAMILY HIKE
EASY

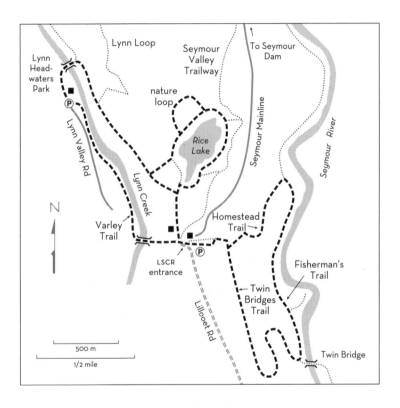

THE SEYMOUR VALLEY below the Seymour Reservoir was opened to the public in 1987, and it is now used for both recreation and forest management activities. The area provides a habitat for a variety of wildlife, including deer, coyote, black bear and cougar, and offers more than 40 km (25 miles) of trails and logging roads for hiking. The low-level route described is particularly suitable for a cold winter's day, the old roads and well-made trails lending themselves to a brisk pace.

> GETTING THERE Vehicle access to the reserve is by Lillooet Road (north) in North Vancouver. The hike described here, however, begins beside Lynn Creek in Lynn Headwaters Regional Park. From Highway 1/99 (Upper Levels Highway), take exit 21, turn right (north) on Mountain Highway and right on Lynn Valley Road. Go straight ahead where Dempsey Road forks left and continue on the winding road to its end at the main parking lot—or use one of the overflow parking lots if necessary.

Although this starting point cannot be reached by public transit, you could take the Lynn Valley bus #228 from Lonsdale Quay SeaBus Terminal to Lynn Valley Road and Dempsey Road. Walk north on Lynn Valley Road (Intake Road), go right on Rice Lake Road and watch for signs for Varley Trail, on which you can join the hiking route. For up-to-date information, contact TransLink at 604-953-3333 or visit their website at translink.ca.

> THE TRAIL Start by crossing to the east side of Lynn Creek and walking downstream (south) on the gravel road. Where the Lynn Loop Trail branches left, you stay to the right along the road to head for the reserve.

After about 15 minutes of walking, take the Rice Lake Loop Trail to your left to begin a clockwise circuit of this attractive, though human-assisted, body of water. An additional short nature loop on the west side of the lake can be incorporated if you wish. Follow the lakeshore trail around the tip of the lake, passing the Seymour Valley Trailway and, in due course, a wharf with a sheltered platform. Stay with the loop trail, turning left at a T-junction and left again when you re-encounter the gravel road from Lynn Headwaters.

Soon, you emerge at the entrance to the reserve. Make for the centre green and follow the signpost for Twin Bridges Trail. After walking alongside a parking lot, continue on the gravel path through two wooden stiles to a T-junction. Turn right. Passing Homestead Trail on your left—your return route—you can now step out along

Twin Bridges Trail as it descends gently through typical coastal forest to the Seymour River.

Arriving at the blue twin bridge, follow Fisherman's Trail left, upstream, on the west bank. After seven or eight minutes of walking, an unmarked, wide gravel trail on the right leads to a delightful picnic spot at a bend in the river—a good place to have lunch and watch dippers among the pools and eddies. Next on Fisherman's Trail are some spawning channels, after which you must turn left and brace yourself for a stiff pull up Homestead to rejoin Twin Bridges Trail and retrace your steps to the reserve entrance.

To find the final leg of your circuit, make your way across the centre green and downhill to your left, following signs for the footbridge across Lynn Creek. Turn right at the end of the bridge and, in a short distance, you'll spot signs for Varley Trail (named in honour of artist Frederick Varley) leading you to a riverside path, enhanced in places by sturdy boardwalks. Staircases lead to overflow parking lots. At trail's end is Lynn Headwaters Park, from which you set forth on your two-river ramble.

VANCOUVER LOOKOUT

Round trip 6 km (3³⁄4 miles)   **Allow** 2¹⁄2 hours
High point 550 m (1800 feet)   Best April to November
Elevation gain 300 m   **MODERATELY EASY**
(900 feet)

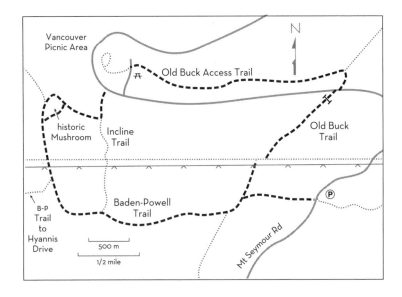

THIS ROUNDABOUT JOURNEY on the forested lower slopes of Mount Seymour Provincial Park uses part of the Baden-Powell Trail to link up with older Mount Seymour trails. The circuit includes the site of the historic "Mushroom," once the meeting place and parking lot for hikers and skiers, and has for its midpoint Vancouver Picnic Area—originally known as Vancouver Lookout, until the forest gradually obscured the view.

> GETTING THERE To reach the starting point, leave Highway 1 in North Vancouver at Mount Seymour exit 22 and stay right onto Mount Seymour Parkway. Opposite Parkgate Centre, a B.C. Parks

sign directs you left on Mount Seymour Road, on which you drive for 2.5 km (1½ miles) beyond the park entrance to a small parking area on the right, opposite a Baden-Powell Trail sign.

> THE TRAIL From the west side of the road, follow the Baden-Powell markers along the well-groomed path for about 400 m (¼ mile) to a junction with the Old Buck Trail. Turn left and in a short distance turn right (west) to continue on the Baden-Powell, now a stony old road. After about 35 minutes of walking, you will come to a signpost indicating the departure of the Baden-Powell for Hyannis Drive. Keep to the right here and you will soon cross a powerline right-of-way with a partial view westward to West Vancouver, Point Atkinson, Bowen Island and beyond.

Follow the red markers into the forest, take the right fork where the trail splits and in a few minutes you will arrive at the Mushroom parking lot. After perusing the history of this bygone meeting place, continue eastward to join Incline Trail, where a sign to the picnic area directs you up the steep track to Mount Seymour Road. Across the road and a few metres downhill is the entrance to the picnic area.

When you are ready to take up your circuit again, head eastward from the parking lot on the Old Buck Access Trail. This picturesque trail, descending gently through stately Douglas-firs, roughly parallels the road to meet the Old Buck Trail. Turn right and descend to Mount Seymour Road.

Walk a little way uphill to pick up the trail on the opposite side, beyond the gate. On this wide track you continue southward, re-crossing the powerline, until you meet again the Baden-Powell Trail branching left—your outward route, leading you back to Mount Seymour Road and your car.

DOG MOUNTAIN

Round trip 6 km (3³/₄ miles)   Best July to October

Allow 2¹/₂ hours   **EASY**

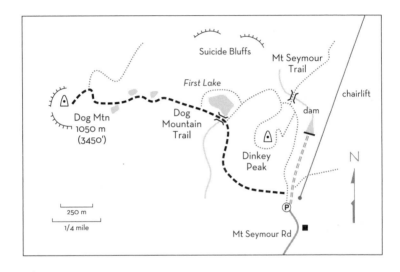

Suicide Bluffs

Mt Seymour Trail

First Lake

chairlift

Dog Mtn
1050 m
(3450')

Dog
Mountain
Trail

dam

Dinkey
Peak

N

250 m

1/4 mile

Mt Seymour Rd

FOR A DAY when you haven't much time but feel like a taste of
the mountains, Dog Mountain in Mount Seymour Provincial Park
is ideal. Only a short drive from the city, this hike can be done easily in a half day, provided you can manage a rough trail. Boots are
recommended. Be prepared for muddy spots and take care on the
summit bluffs, as the drop-off is very steep. These open bluffs give
a fine mountaintop feeling and offer good views of the city and the
Seymour River Valley.

Dog Mountain is not worth attempting before July, for ice and
snow linger in this region. Choose a clear day and, as with all Mount
Seymour trips, take insect repellent.

> GETTING THERE From Highway 1 in North Vancouver, take
Mount Seymour exit 22 and keep right onto Mount Seymour

Parkway. Opposite Parkgate Centre, a B.C. Parks sign directs you left on Mount Seymour Road, which you follow to its end at the ski area. Park at the north end of the lot.

> **THE TRAIL** Walk north on the gravel path for a few metres to find the signpost for Dog Mountain and First Lake, directing you left into the forest. The trail is marked with red metal markers. In 20 minutes you cross the outlet stream of First Lake, where you may want to rest for a few minutes before following the trail along the lake's south shore.

After re-entering the woods, the path becomes rougher and perhaps wetter for the next 20 minutes as you pick your way through an area of small ponds before gaining height.

About an hour from the start, you should reach Dog Mountain's rocky summit, with its views of the Seymour River Valley to the west, Lions Gate Bridge, Stanley Park and Point Grey to the southwest. These views may appear and disappear before your eyes, for even in fine weather, clouds often drift across the slopes of Mount Seymour. Beds of delicate saxifrage bloom on the bluffs, as does copperbush, recognizable by the hooked green anthers protruding from the centres of the coppery-pink flowers.

Leaving, don't be tempted by the taped route heading left from the base of the bluff—it's a challenging and hazardous trail unsuitable for "easy hikers." Simply retrace your steps.

MYSTERY LAKE

Round trip 5 km (3 miles)   Best July to October
High point 1170 m (3850 feet)   FAMILY HIKE
Elevation gain 180 m (600 feet)   **MODERATELY EASY**
Allow 3 hours

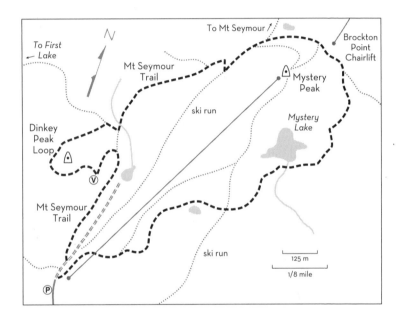

IF THE CHALLENGING five-hour hike to Mount Seymour's three peaks is more than you care to tackle, this modest circular trip will give you, for less effort, a sampling of the mountain's subalpine lakes and flora and views from rocky outcroppings. Choose a fine day (do not attempt any hike on Mount Seymour in bad weather) and wait until the snow has gone—Seymour trails are rugged enough without the added hazard of melting snow. Wear boots and keep markers in sight at all times. During July and August, you may be glad of insect repellent or protective clothing.

Mystery Lake

> **GETTING THERE** Prepared but not deterred, leave Highway 1 in
North Vancouver at Mount Seymour exit 22 and keep right onto
Mount Seymour Parkway. Opposite Parkgate Centre, a B.C. Parks
sign directs you left on Mount Seymour Road, which you follow to
its end at the parking lot at the ski area.

> **THE TRAIL** From the north end of the parking lot, you set off on
the main Mount Seymour Alpine Trail, veering left after passing the
signpost for Dog Mountain. After about 15 minutes of climbing, look
out for the signpost to Dinkey Peak, for this is the start of a minor
loop well worth including in your itinerary for its rewarding viewpoints. The first of these, won by climbing a wooden ladder onto a
rocky bluff, affords a view south to the Fraser delta and west across
the Strait of Georgia. Continuing on the loop trail (keep the yellow and orange markers in sight), you wander over subsequent bluffs
from which you can gaze upon the three peaks of Mount Seymour
before descending to meet a trail from First Lake. Keep straight
ahead at this junction to rejoin Mount Seymour Alpine Trail and
resume your northward progress.

Soon the trail ascends right to join a ski run for a short distance. Where the run swings right to the chairlift terminal, you keep straight ahead to a parting of the ways. Leaving Mount Seymour Alpine Trail to continue northward past a small pond, you go uphill to the right.

Now climbing around the back of Mystery Peak, you soon arrive at the lower terminal of the Brockton Point chairlift, from where Mystery Lake Trail branches right to begin its descent to the lake. This rough, and often damp, stretch of trail, fringed by partridge foot and Indian hellebore, eventually rises among heathery meadow patches and small ponds before arriving at peaceful Mystery Lake cradled by rocky promontories. There are picnic and swimming spots to choose from, and outcroppings to the east offer views of the city and Burrard Inlet.

Rested and refreshed, follow the marked, rocky trail downhill, crossing a ski run and passing diminutive Nancy Lake on the way, until you emerge once again at the foot of the Mystery Peak chairlift within sight of your transport.

GREY ROCK

Round trip 5 km (3 miles)   **Allow** 2½ hours
High point 200 m (660 feet)   Good most of the year
Elevation gain 180 m (600 feet) **MODERATELY EASY**

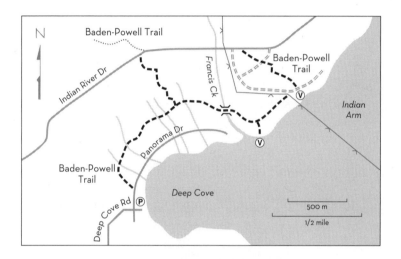

THIS EASTERNMOST SECTION of the 40-km (25-mile) Baden-Powell Trail provides an invigorating walk for most times of year. Steps and bridges help you across the many ravines scoring Mount Seymour's lower flank. Your destination is a rocky bluff overlooking Indian Arm. Try for a clear day.

> GETTING THERE In North Vancouver, take Mount Seymour Parkway or Dollarton Highway to Deep Cove. Turn left on Panorama Drive and leave your car in the public parking lot on the right. Walk along Panorama Drive, or through the park, and you will see the beginning of the Baden-Powell Trail heading up steps to the left of the road.

This starting point can be reached by public transit: Take the Deep Cove bus #212 from Phibbs Exchange to Panorama Drive. For up-to-date information, contact TransLink at 604-953-3333 or visit their website at translink.ca.

> THE TRAIL After a steep beginning, the well-marked trail swings northeast through a series of fern-clad ravines. Some striking examples of large trees growing out of nurse stumps can be seen along the way. After about 40 minutes of up-and-down progress, you will cross a powerline before descending to the bridge over Francis Creek. A final short climb brings you to a fork in the trail.

The right-hand path leads to the pine-treed bluff—a good lunch spot with views of Deep Cove, Belcarra and Indian Arm—or you can keep left for a further five minutes to emerge onto the B.C. Hydro right-of-way, where, from below the last pylon, you can enjoy a view across the water to Buntzen Ridge and Eagle Ridge beyond.

From here you may be content to return directly to Deep Cove, but if you wish to add variety to the walk by making a partial loop, then look for the marked Baden-Powell Trail heading into the forest a short distance beyond the powerline right-of-way. After about 10 minutes of climbing, you will come to a dirt road on which you must walk left for a few metres to pick up the continuation of the Baden-Powell. In a few more minutes you will emerge onto Indian River Drive.

Go left (west) on this paved road for about 400 m (¼ mile). A few metres beyond where the Baden-Powell heads into the woods on the right, you will notice a fire hydrant. Opposite this, markers indicate the beginning of an old trail descending steeply through the forest to rejoin your outward route to the bluff.

Turn right, of course, when you meet the Baden-Powell, to retrace your steps through the tall firs and hemlocks to your Deep Cove starting point.

BLUE GENTIAN LAKE

Round trip 9 km (5½ miles)
High point 800 m (2600 feet)
Elevation gain 450 m
(1450 feet)

Allow 4½ hours
Best May to November
MODERATELY EASY

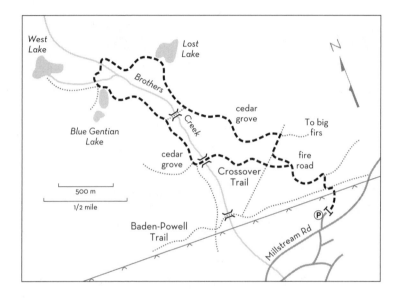

YOU WILL WALK among giants on this lower Hollyburn circuit. Two groves of large western red cedars and many ancient stumps bearing sawyers' notches are reminders of the forest as it once was. In late fall, a fascinating variety of fungi can be seen in the woods, and the two small lakes, much frequented in summer, will now be left to themselves—and you.

> GETTING THERE Drive north on Taylor Way in West Vancouver and turn left at the roundabout onto Southborough Drive. At the first four-way stop, turn left onto Highland Drive. Stay on Highland until you reach Eyremount Drive, where you turn left again.

Brothers Creek fire road in winter

In about 800 m (½ mile) swing right onto Millstream Road and continue uphill on Millstream for a further kilometre to where a spur road branches uphill to the left. Park here, respecting the prohibited areas.

Although this starting point cannot be reached by public transit, you could take the British Properties bus #254 from Park Royal to Crestwell Road and Eyremount Drive and walk via Henlow and Millstream to the starting point. For up-to-date information, contact TransLink at 604-953-3333 or visit their website at translink.ca.

> THE TRAIL Go through the gate onto the signposted Brothers Creek Fire Road. After a short distance the wide track bears left and is joined by the Baden-Powell Trail as far as the powerline. At this point, the fire road, also signed Brothers Creek Forestry Heritage Walk, ascends straight ahead into the woods, marked with red metal squares. This is your route.

After passing the trail to Ballantree on the right, you begin to climb steadily. About a half hour's walking from the start, you will see Crossover Trail joining from the left—this will be your return route; for now, you press on, following the fire road and Brothers

Creek Forestry Heritage Walk signs as you toil upward. Soon after a sharp right turn onto an old cable railway, you part company with the Forestry Heritage Walk and stay left with the fire road as it levels off somewhat and enters a stretch of old forest. Western hemlock and amabilis fir tower on either side. After crossing a stream, you pass through an extensive grove of western red cedar, at the end of which you emerge into a glade beside a bridge spanning Brothers Creek.

Stay on the east side of the creek, climbing for a further 400 m (¼ mile) to Lost Lake. A short side trail leads to this attractive little lake. Returning to the main trail, follow the B.C. Parks markers westward along the rough trail to Blue Gentian Lake. After bypassing three broken bridges and passing through some swampy patches, the trail climbs to a precipitous viewpoint (now overgrown) above Brothers Creek upper falls before descending to cross the creek itself. Some boulder-hopping may be necessary here. Stoney Creek too, must be crossed, beyond which you will arrive at a signed trail junction. Go left to Blue Gentian Lake.

In early summer, this sequestered little lake is adorned with water lilies and buckbean plants. Swamp laurel blooms at its edge, and mats of deer cabbage grow along the rivulets of the marsh. In August, deep blue king gentians bloom en masse beside the boardwalk.

Having rested at the lone picnic table, continue along the lake's eastern shore to begin your return journey. It is an easy half hour's descent through semi-open forest back to the bridge over Brothers Creek. To complete the circuit, stay on the west side of the creek. There are glimpses of the gorge and its waterfalls as for the next 800 m (½ mile) you descend quite steeply with the aid of wooden stairs and bridges—some of which may be in need of repair.

After passing through another grove of giant cedars, watch for the junction with Crossover Trail, where you go left down to a footbridge over Brothers Creek. It is now a 20-minute walk through second-growth forest, crossing the old cable railway on your way, to rejoin the fire road, along which you retrace your steps to the gate off Millstream Road.

FORKS-SKYLINE CIRCUIT

Round trip 7 km (4½ miles)
High point 650 m (2100 feet)
Elevation gain 270 m
(900 feet)

Allow 3 hours
Best May to November
MODERATELY EASY

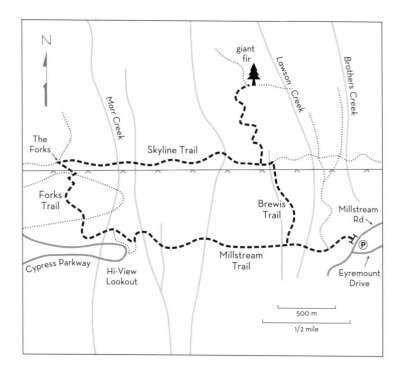

THIS SHORT CIRCUIT on lower Hollyburn is satisfying for its variety, incorporating a stretch of the Baden-Powell Trail, the old Forks Trail and a piece of West Vancouver's Forestry Heritage Walk. The Forks Trail can be reached from Cypress Parkway, but by starting the hike from the British Properties, the climbing is accomplished first and the junction known as The Forks can be your

At the giant Hollyburn Fir

lunch-break objective—appropriately enough, as The Forks was the site of a restaurant in bygone days, along the old Hollyburn chairlift.

If time and energy allow, a worthwhile side trip can be included to visit one of Vancouver's largest trees. Standing 45 m (150 feet) high and almost 3 m (10 feet) in diameter, this giant Douglas-fir is thought to be nearly 1100 years old. Allow an extra 30 minutes for this side trip.

> GETTING THERE Leave Highway 1/99 (Upper Levels Highway) in West Vancouver at exit 13, drive north on Taylor Way and turn left at the roundabout onto Southborough Drive. At the first four-way stop, turn left onto Highland Drive. Stay on Highland until you reach Eyremount Drive, where you turn left again. Where Eyremount meets Millstream Road on a sharp bend, you will spot a

gated road and a marker indicating access to the Baden-Powell Trail. Park here.

Although this starting point cannot be reached by public transit, you could take the British Properties bus #254 to Crestwell Road and Eyremount Drive and walk south on Eyremount to the starting point. For up-to-date information, contact TransLink at 604-953-3333 or visit their website at translink.ca.

> THE TRAIL Heading westward from the barrier, stay on Millstream Trail at the next junction, cross the bridge over Lawson Creek and watch for the Forestry signpost "Brewis Trail" on your right. Although steep, this path is soft underfoot as it wends its way through the forest to the Baden-Powell Skyline Trail—about a half hour's climb.

Here begins the westward leg of your circuit. In only a few minutes, you will see the signposted Brewis Trail continuing northward; this is the route to the giant Hollyburn Fir. Be careful to keep the small triangle markers in sight on this trail. After the side trip, retrace your steps and continue west along Skyline Trail.

For about 40 minutes, you follow the well-marked path (now part of the Trans Canada Trail) along its alternating open stretches and forest glades, dropping occasionally into ravines to cross the several creeks that flow from Hollyburn into Burrard Inlet. Arriving eventually at the four-way Forks junction, backtrack a few steps to find your route descending from the Trans Canada signpost just east of the junction.

This old hikers' trail is rough and steep in places as it descends in a somewhat southeasterly direction toward Cypress Parkway at HiView Lookout. Yellow or red markers help to keep you on route through the maze of mountain-bike tracks. The descent continues to a small bridge over Marr Creek. Shortly after this, watch for an unmarked trail to the left. There is a British Pacific Properties sign on a tree at this point. A wire fence and gate are visible to your right; HiView Lookout can be glimpsed through the trees. Follow the left-hand path as it descends steeply to cross a creek, and then a second one, before joining an old road. The last leg of your journey is mostly level walking as you follow Millstream Trail back to your starting point.

HOLLYBURN LAKES

Round trip 7 km (4½ miles)   **Allow** 3 hours
High point 950 m (3100 feet)   Good June to October
Elevation gain 150 m (500 feet) **MODERATELY EASY**

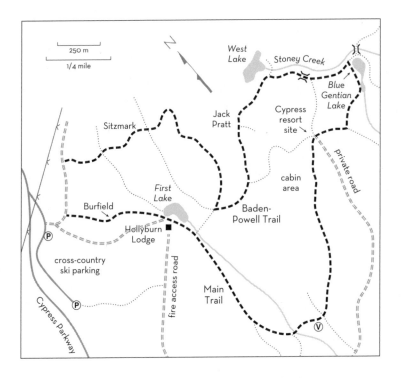

HERE IS A short up-and-down hike among lower Hollyburn's honey-comb of trails, combining old hiking routes with cross-country ski trails. The circuit includes three of the mountain's numerous lakes and passes through many a blueberry patch—a bonus if you go in August, as are the king gentians that bloom around Blue Gentian Lake at that time.

King gentians

> **GETTING THERE** Leave Highway 1/99 (Upper Levels Highway) in West Vancouver at the Cypress Bowl exit 8. Drive up Cypress Parkway for about 13 km (8 miles) and turn off to the right to the parking lot for the cross-country (Nordic) ski area. Park at the north end of the lot.

> **THE TRAIL** Begin by climbing the track beneath the powerline. In about 400 m (¼ mile), branch off to the right on Sitzmark Trail, staying with this as it crosses Telemark and Wells Gray Trails (the latter is also the Baden-Powell Trail and part of the Trans Canada Trail) before turning southward to a major four-way junction. Head left (east) now, on the Grand National, but fork left again in about 200 m (220 yards) onto Jack Pratt. Stay left where Jack Pratt branches right and descend through the trees to West Lake.

Look now for a sign to Blue Gentian Lake. This next section of trail is fairly steep and rough as it descends beside Stoney Creek, but it does offer glimpses of the canyon below. Immediately after crossing a bridge over a ravine, you'll see a sign directing you left to Blue Gentian Lake. A subsequent right turn brings you to the secluded lake in its marshy setting.

The right-hand path and boardwalk along the west side of the lake is your route. Turn right when you meet the Baden-Powell Trail and proceed through the woods until you arrive at the clearing where Cypress Resort once stood. This is not a place of beauty, so head for the stony track to the right of the more obvious private road descending southward from the clearing. The track soon becomes a well-defined trail through the forest; several cabins add interest along the way.

Once the main hiking and ski approach to Hollyburn, this trail makes pleasant walking and brings you in less than 2 km (1¼ miles) to another reminder of bygone days—the site of the old HiView Lodge and chairlift terminal. Although the view over the city has grown in, a bench invites a rest or lunch break if you resisted the charms of Blue Gentian Lake.

After crossing Marr Creek, continue along the trail in its north-westerly direction until you join another well-used hiking trail on which you turn right (north) toward First Lake and Hollyburn Lodge. Copious blueberry bushes might detain you here, but to return to your car at the cross-country parking, locate the Burfield Trail heading northwest from the lake. Thus you complete one of many possible circuits among Hollyburn's network of trails.

HOLLYBURN MOUNTAIN

Round trip 8 km (5 miles)   **Allow** 3½ hours
High point 1325 m (4350 feet)   Best July to October
Elevation gain 400 m   **MODERATELY EASY**
(1300 feet)

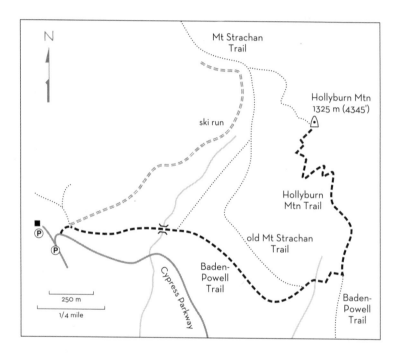

SEEN FROM VANCOUVER, modest Hollyburn Mountain displays no peak, so the open summit, with its tarn and good views to the north and east, may come as a pleasant surprise. By starting the hike from the Cypress Bowl downhill ski area, an attractive stretch of the Baden-Powell Trail can be used to connect with the Hollyburn Mountain Trail.

> GETTING THERE From Highway 1/99 (Upper Levels Highway) in West Vancouver, take the Cypress Park exit 8. Drive Cypress Parkway to its end at the downhill ski area.

> THE TRAIL Due to reconstruction of the downhill ski area for the 2010 Olympics, some hiking trails have been re-routed. From the roadside information kiosk, walk north past the first aid and ski patrol building to a signpost indicating the Baden-Powell Trail heading right (east) into the forest. Thereafter, the trail is marked with the usual orange metal markers.

At first you climb steadily as you traverse the forested slope, crossing numerous little creeks on sometimes slippery bridges. After toiling thus for about 40 minutes, you will pass the old Mount Strachan Trail on your left, and a further 10 minutes of walking will bring you to the junction with the Hollyburn Mountain Trail. Turning left (north) now, you follow the zigzag path, sometimes in the open amid blueberry and huckleberry bushes, sometimes through the forest. After about a half hour's climb, watch for a viewpoint with a bench a few metres to the right of the trail on a sharp left bend. Here, while catching your breath, you can gaze across the Capilano Valley to the peaks beyond.

The trail continues steeply for a short distance then opens out into a heathery meadow, where you may be tempted to eat your lunch among the rocks and pools. The summit, however, is only 20 minutes away and worth the extra effort involved.

Leaving the meadow, the route is fairly obvious, though not well marked. It takes you over some rock slabs, up a staircase of roots and along a rocky ledge, until, after a final scramble, you step out onto the summit plateau. To the north, you can see Mount Strachan and the Lions, and to the east, on a clear day, Grouse, Goat and Crown Mountains.

Return to Cypress Bowl by reversing your outward route.

YEW LAKE AND BOWEN LOOKOUT

Round trip 4 km (2½ miles);
Yew Lake Loop only 2 km
(1¼ miles)
Allow 2½ hours
Best July to October

Wheelchair accessible Yew Lake
Loop Trail only
FAMILY HIKE (Yew Lake Loop)
EASY

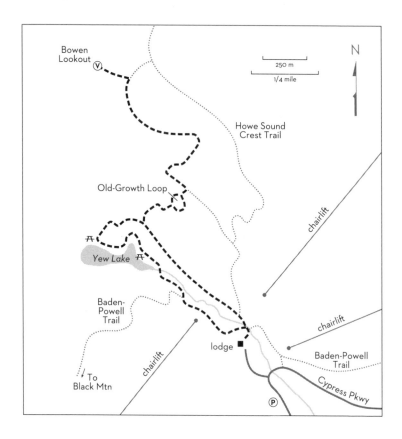

Rowan berries

HIKERS SHOULD NOT consider the short, wheelchair-accessible Yew Lake Loop beneath their notice; it is a magical walk that follows Cypress Creek through thickets of white-flowered rhododendrons, between banks of heather and hellebore and blueberry shrubs, to the creek's source in a subalpine lake. This tranquil waterway, swollen by other mountain streams, later cascades down through Cypress Falls Park (see Hike 34) on its way to Burrard Inlet. The trail continues through sedge meadows to a surprising remnant of old-growth forest. Interpretative panels add interest; a detailed leaflet is available from the visitor centre in the lodge. Those not deterred by some climbing can lengthen the outing to include a new trail to a stunning viewpoint—Bowen Lookout.

> GETTING THERE Leave Highway 1/99 (Upper Levels Highway) in West Vancouver, at the Cypress Park exit 8. Drive Cypress Parkway to its end at the downhill ski area.

> THE TRAIL From the information kiosk east of Cypress Creek Lodge, follow Yew Lake signs, staying left where the trail forks to begin a clockwise circuit. After passing the base of the Eagle

chairlift and a new section of the Baden-Powell Trail branching left to Black Mountain plateau, you will cross a bridge over Cypress Creek, beyond which the lower part of Yew Lake soon comes into sight. A picnic table ahead provides a good spot to pause beside this peaceful, secluded lake nestled below the northern flank of Black Mountain.

From here the path leaves the lake to meander through sub-alpine meadows and around ponds to arrive at a trail junction; go left here and left again to enter the old-growth forest. Pass by the fallen mountain hemlock and walk beneath stately yellow cedars and ama-bilis firs until you see a minor trail heading northeast between two tall hemlocks. This is your route to Bowen Lookout.

The path soon emerges onto an old road, on which you turn left. In a few minutes, you'll reach a new bridge and a gravelled trail striking off to the right. On this, you wend your way upward to a signpost directing you left to Bowen Lookout. After a short descent, you'll step out onto a wide platform with, before you, a sweeping panorama of Howe Sound, Bowen, Gambier and Anvil Islands and the Sunshine Coast mountains beyond.

It is not easy to tear yourself away from this scenic extrava-ganza, but eventually you will need to retrace your steps to the Old-Growth Loop. Turn left as you re-enter the forest and left to rejoin the remaining leg of the Yew Lake Loop Trail. Heading homeward through the wetland area, you may be able to spot butterwort and insect-eating sundew plants. All too soon, you find yourself re-crossing Cypress Creek, with the lodge and ski facilities before you.

BLACK MOUNTAIN

Round trip 7.5 km (4³/4 miles)   **Allow** 5 hours
High point 1200 m (4000 feet)   Best June to October
Elevation gain 300 m   **MODERATELY DIFFICULT**
(1000 feet)

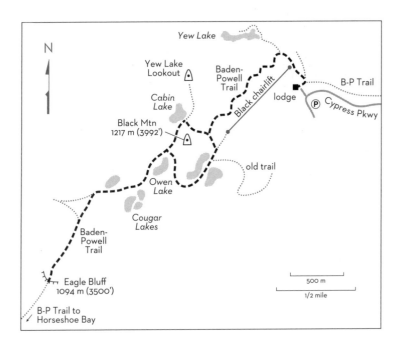

A STRING OF subalpine lakes, magnificent views and a swim in cool, clear water are among the rewards for those who bear with the first trying 45 minutes of this hike. Many will be content to explore Cabin Lake and the mountain's two peaks, but it is a pity to miss spectacular Eagle Bluff on the mountain's southwest tip—the route described here. The Black Mountain plateau is usually accessible in June, sometimes earlier, and offers good walking until late fall.

Cabin Lake

> **GETTING THERE** From Highway 1/99 (Upper Levels Highway) in West Vancouver, take the Cypress Park exit 8. Drive Cypress Parkway to its end at the downhill ski area.

> **THE TRAIL** Expansion of the downhill ski area for the 2010 Olympics has resulted in the re-routing of the Baden-Powell Trail. Now you must walk past the new lodge to find a signpost to Yew Lake and the Baden-Powell Trail to Black Mountain. Proceed past the base of the Black chairlift until you come to another signpost directing you left and uphill to Black Mountain. Brace yourself for a stiff climb and soldier on. Keeping west of the ski area, you will eventually pass a small lake, beyond which a stone staircase brings you to a trail junction. If your objective is Eagle Bluff, go left with the Baden-Powell, passing up, for the moment, the summit of Black Mountain. If your destination is Cabin Lake and Black Mountain only, turn right and follow the boardwalk to the lake.

On to Eagle Bluff: From the top of the chairlift follow the Baden-Powell, passing on your way the former, now disused, route to your left. On a path bordered by cotton sedge and heather and meadow spirea, you pass between two subalpine lakes to a meeting with the trail from Black Mountain summit—your return route. Turn left at this signposted junction and follow the Baden-Powell as it winds among a series of small lakes. The first, Owen Lake, is scattered with islands; another, half-moon shaped, is part of the Cougar Lakes group; next comes Turtle Lake, named for its humpbacked rocks. After passing Upper Lake on the right, the trail descends steeply over rocks. Two side trails to the right are passed, and finally, after about two and a half hours of walking from the start, you emerge onto Eagle Bluff.

Now there are expansive views of Howe Sound and the Gulf Islands, with Horseshoe Bay just below you. Cushions of kinnikinnick, clumps of penstemon and clusters of tiger lilies, lupines and twinflower decorate the bluff.

From here the Baden-Powell Trail drops very steeply among the boulders below the bluff to Horseshoe Bay. This descent is not easy hiking, so you, of course, wisely retrace your steps toward Cypress Bowl. This time, on arriving at the trail junction just beyond Owen Lake, stay left to visit Cabin Lake and the mountain's peaks. It is a 10-minute climb from the junction to Black Mountain's main (south) summit, with its views of Vancouver, Howe Sound and northward to the Lions.

It is a further five-minute walk down to Cabin Lake, an inviting spot for swimming or just sitting. A side trail leads from here to the north summit, also known as Yew Lake Lookout, should you crave more views, in this case of the Lions and the Tantalus Range. From Cabin Lake, the boardwalk returns you to the top of the chairlift, ready for the steep descent on the Baden-Powell to Cypress Bowl.

HOWE SOUND CREST

Round trip 11 km (7 miles)
High point 1330 m (4400 feet)
Elevation gain 430 m
(1400 feet)

Allow 5 hours
Best July to October
MODERATELY DIFFICULT

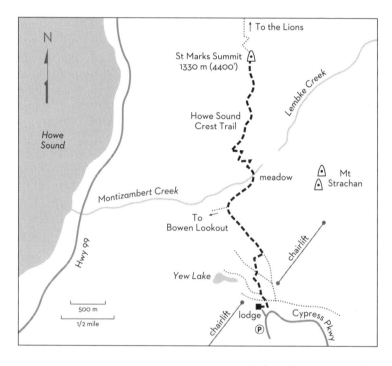

HOWE SOUND CREST TRAIL, once an informal route along the ridge above Howe Sound, is today a scenic 30-km (20-mile) trail to the Lions and beyond, providing a challenging, high-level hike for experienced backpackers. A modest sampling of the route, for day hikers, is this 11-km (7-mile) round trip to St. Marks Summit. The excursion is best made from July onwards to avoid old snow patches and is suitable for even a warm day, as most of the climbing is in the shade of the forest.

The Lions from St. Mark's summit

> **GETTING THERE** From Highway 1/99 (Upper Levels Highway) in West Vancouver, take the Cypress Park exit 8. Drive Cypress Parkway to its end at the downhill ski area.

> **THE TRAIL** Reconstruction of the ski area for the 2010 Olympics has resulted in some changes to hiking trails. Walk past the new Cypress Creek Lodge to your right to find a signpost for Yew Lake Trail and Old-Growth Loop. Staying on the east side of Cypress Creek, follow the Yew Lake Trail for a short distance to the next signpost directing you right on Howe Sound Crest Trail. On reaching Pumphouse Road, go left for a few metres, then right at the trail sign and head uphill through the forest on a rough trail, from which you emerge on another gravel road above the Yew Lake valley; turn left here and continue to the road's end, where a foot trail heads into the forest proper.

About a half hour's walking from the start, a short side trail on the left leads to Bowen Lookout (see Hike 31). Just beyond this junction, the Lions can be seen from the main trail.

The trail now winds along the steep side hill of Mount Strachan, crossing Montizambert Creek, before opening out into a sheltered meadow. This is a peaceful spot for a rest, conveniently halfway to your destination. Valerian, hellebore, arnica and asters cluster around the stream, while the twin peaks of Mount Strachan stand guard over the valley.

Refreshed, you start up the series of switchbacks that will take you to the ridge overlooking Howe Sound—about a half hour's climbing. As you walk north along the ridge, minor paths lead to viewpoints and meadow patches. St. Marks Summit can be glimpsed straight ahead.

Next is a short descent, followed by the final climb to the summit. Assisted by switchbacks and steps, you reach the first heathery meadows of St. Marks, after which the trail continues more gently to a pond on the summit, where your reward awaits you.

To the north, beyond the aptly named hump of Unnecessary Mountain, stand the Lions, Mount Harvey and Mount Brunswick. To the west lie the islands of Howe Sound. (Take care approaching this precipitous viewpoint.) Mount Seymour and Grouse and Crown Mountains can be seen through the trees from the knoll east of the pond. Most will agree that St. Marks makes a satisfactory turnaround point for a day on Howe Sound Crest.

CYPRESS FALLS PARK

Round trip 3 km (2 miles)　　　Good all year
Allow 1½ hours　　　**MODERATELY EASY**

THIS BEAUTIFUL, LITTLE-KNOWN park along Cypress Creek offers year-round walking through undisturbed old-growth forest, with waterfall and creekside views. In summer, you might spot coral-root orchids and Indian pipe growing around the feet of the giant cedars and 400-year-old Douglas-firs. Later in the year, colourful mushrooms bloom from the forest floor.

The short, but energetic, hike makes use of a service road to explore both west and east sides of Cypress Creek. The route is steep in places, with roots and rocks underfoot and some risky drop-offs. Although at present the trails are unmarked (this may change), the creek itself can be an aid to navigation, as it tumbles southward through its narrow canyon.

> GETTING THERE From Highway 1/99 (Upper Levels Highway) in West Vancouver, take the Caulfeild-Woodgreen Drive exit 4. Turn right at the stop sign and right again at Woodgreen Place. Go left into the upper parking area.

This starting point can be reached by public transit: Take the Caulfeild bus #253 from Park Royal and alight at Woodgreen Place and Woodgreen Drive. For up-to-date information, contact Trans-Link at 604-953-3333 or visit their website at translink.ca.

> THE TRAIL Begin by crossing the parking lot and following the trail left and uphill into the forest. After a few minutes of climbing, take the trail descending on the right—an old pipeline route that hugs the benchland above Cypress Creek. After a breathtaking view of the Lower Falls, you must clamber up to the left to join the main trail. Do not cross the bridge at Lower Falls—this is your return route.

A 30-minute climb beneath majestic Douglas-firs, hemlocks and cedars brings you to a viewpoint below the Upper Falls, after which the trail levels off to meet a fire access road. Turn right on this gravel road and right again to cross Cypress Creek on the sturdy McCrady Bridge. Walk down the service road past a B.C. Hydro substation and a school board workshop. Ignore a hydro service road on the left and continue downhill toward a bend, where a "Trail" sign directs you to the right.

Soon you are back in the forest, descending through another grove of old-growth trees to the bridge above Lower Falls. On the west side of the creek, climb the bank to join the main trail and follow this higher route left and downhill back to the parking area—well tried in leg and lung.

EAGLE CREEK RAMBLE

Round trip 6.5 km (4 miles)   **Allow** 3½ hours
High point 460 m (1500 feet)   Good most of the year
Elevation gain 420 m   **MODERATELY EASY**
(1380 feet)

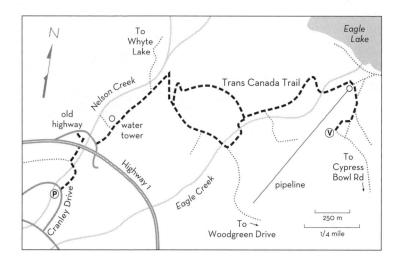

THIS CHALLENGING LITTLE hike largely follows the Trans Canada Trail as it ventures onto the mountain slopes below Cypress Provincial Park. From a beginning steeped in road and railway history, the route passes through the once-restricted area of Nelson Canyon, crosses and re-crosses Eagle Creek and culminates at an unsuspected viewpoint. The outing is satisfying as a winter workout or as a leisurely ramble at any time of year.

> GETTING THERE In West Vancouver, follow Marine Drive westward and turn right on Cranley Drive in the 5700 block. In about 400 m (¼ mile), locate the Trans Canada Trail sign on the right and park where convenient at the side of the road.

Viewpoint bluff

Although this starting point cannot be reached by public transit, you could take the Horseshoe Bay bus #250 from Park Royal and alight near Marine Drive and Cranley Drive and walk to the starting point. For up-to-date information, contact TransLink at 604-953-3333 or visit their website at translink.ca.

> **THE TRAIL** After crossing Nelson Creek on a footbridge, you climb to an old railway right-of-way, now Seaview Walk—a delightful route to Horseshoe Bay via the Trans Canada Trail's western segment. Today's excursion calling for sterner stuff, you must follow the Trans Canada Trail east and upward, passing beneath Highway 1 to step out on the abandoned roadbed of the old Upper Levels Highway. Walk to the right, re-crossing Nelson Creek, to find the trail heading north from the east end of the bridge.

After ascending to a water tower, you strike off to the right on a foot trail and soon you are climbing beneath magnificent Douglas-firs and cedars high above the Nelson canyon. Stay right with the Trans Canada Trail where Whyte Lake Trail (see Hike 36) branches left. After a final stairway, beside which a grand old fir stands guard, the trail levels off as it joins an old forest road.

At the next signpost (K5), follow the trail left, gaining height once more as you tread the forest path. A short side trail on the right, after about 15 minutes of climbing, leads to a partial viewpoint. A few minutes beyond this diversion, your trail converges with Eagle Creek. Note here a trail descending to the right—this could be an alternative return route. For now, press on until you emerge on a pipeline right-of-way below a water tower. Climb around behind the tower, staying faithfully with the Trans Canada Trail to skirt the restricted watershed area, until you reach a fork where a signpost reading "Access to Cypress Bowl Road" directs you onto the right-hand, older road. Immediately beyond the sign, go right again on a minor loop road and watch for a path heading up the bank on your right. (If you rejoin the original road, you've gone too far and missed your viewpoint destination.) A short scramble brings you onto a mossy bluff. Descend a little to the open rock beyond, and you can gaze upon West Vancouver and the city, the Strait of Georgia and the Gulf Islands while enjoying a lunch break.

In due course, backtrack to where the Trans Canada Trail swings uphill away from Eagle Creek and, if you wish, take the trail you noted earlier. After crossing the creek at the base of a looming rock face, the trail descends through mixed woodland to emerge on an old road. On this, you tramp along westward, through second-growth forest with many an ancient stump, and after 15 minutes, you'll find yourself back at a familiar junction, K5, reunited with the Trans Canada Trail for your return to Cranley Drive.

WHYTE LAKE

Round trip 4.6 km (3 miles)
High point 320 m (1050 feet)
Elevation gain 190 m (620 feet)

Allow 2½ hours
Good most of the year
MODERATELY EASY

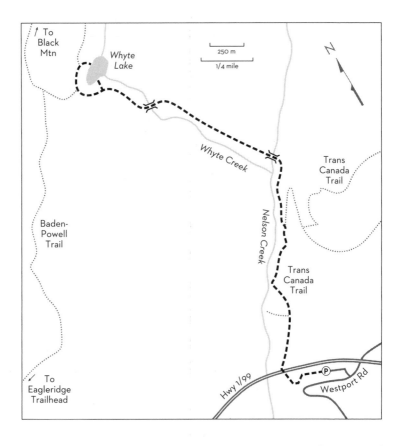

SITUATED IN A watershed area, Whyte Lake was long out of
bounds to hikers. Thanks in part to Highway 1/99 reconstruction,
this has now changed. A new trailhead connects with the Trans
Canada Trail through Nelson Canyon, and an old trail beside

Whyte Creek has been restored. This upgraded trail serves as a connecting route between the Trans Canada Trail and the Baden-Powell Trail, but a there-and-back trip to Whyte Lake makes a satisfying outing on its own. The walk through old-growth forest is breathtaking; the tranquil, tucked-away little lake is a pleasing destination.

> GETTING THERE Leave Highway 1/99 (Upper Levels Highway) at exit 4 and drive west on Westport Road. After passing beneath Highway 1/99, go right on a service road and leave your car in the Whyte Lake Trailhead parking area.

> THE TRAIL Walk past the yellow gate and follow the service road as it passes beneath Highway 1/99. Keep straight ahead at the first Trans Canada Trail sign. At the signpost for Trans Canada Trail (East), turn right on a foot trail into the forest. Accompanied by the sound of Nelson Creek from the canyon below, you climb beneath grand cedars and Douglas-firs to a marked trail junction beside a large cedar stump. Here, saying goodbye to the Trans Canada Trail, you descend left to cross Nelson Creek on a sturdy footbridge. Your trail now follows Whyte Creek upstream through stands of old-growth firs and hemlocks and tumbles of giant boulders. Shortly after crossing the creek, take a short, unmarked trail to the right, which leads to a wooden dock on the south shore of Whyte Lake.

There is more to explore. Returning to the main trail, continue along a series of boardwalks to another trail junction, this one guarded by a tall A-frame outhouse with an unusual stable door. Turn right here (left goes on to join the Baden-Powell Trail on its way from Black Mountain to Horseshoe Bay) and, after a short distance, branch off right again toward the lake. This path ends at a secluded beach—an agreeable place to while away some time. If you rest here in summer, warblers and dragonflies keep you company, swallows skim over the water and leaping fish leave rings on the lake's surface.

When it's time to head homeward, retrace your route around the lake and set off back along the boardwalks and through the enchanted forest to your car at the trailhead.

LIGHTHOUSE PARK

Round trip 5 km (3 miles)

Allow 3 hours

Good all year

FAMILY HIKE (Valley Trail)

EASY

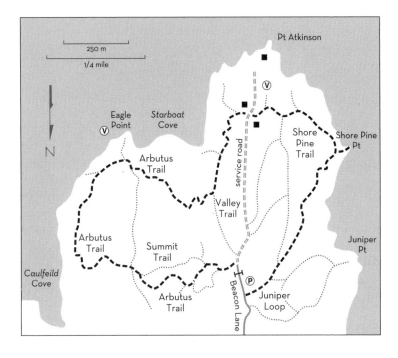

FOR MANY VANCOUVER residents Lighthouse Park has long been a favourite place for walking and picnicking; its main trails at least are well known and well worn. From the profusion of paths and trails criss-crossing the 75 ha (185 acres) of untouched coastal forest forming the backdrop to the Point Atkinson lighthouse, we have devised a circular hike that explores the less-frequented eastern side of the park, as well as the popular west coast. These perimeter trails surmount the highest part of the peninsula and are often rough underfoot, requiring sturdy footwear. Families with small children

Arbutus

might prefer to take the self-guiding nature walk along Valley Trail. Leaflets and maps are usually available at the kiosks in the parking area. Nature lovers will be thrilled by the giant Douglas-firs of the interior valleys and the arbutus, manzanita, mosses and lilies on the headlands and rocky outcrops—a diversity of plant life that reflects the varied topography of the park.

> **GETTING THERE** To reach the park from the West Vancouver end of the Lions Gate Bridge, drive west along Marine Drive for about 10 km (6 miles). A short distance beyond Caulfeild Cove you will see the Lighthouse Park sign directing you left. Follow Beacon Lane to the parking area.

This starting point can be reached by public transit: Take the Horseshoe Bay bus #250 from Park Royal, alight at Marine Drive and Beacon Lane and walk to the park entrance. For up-to-date information, contact TransLink at 604-953-3333 or visit their website at translink.ca.

> **THE TRAIL** Start by going through the metal gate at the south end of the parking lot and immediately head left (east) on a foot trail signposted Salal Loop. Keep right at the next junction, staying thereafter with Arbutus Trail as it continues in an easterly direction toward the coast. Eventually, still on Arbutus, you find yourself following the coastline southward among big trees and past several minor rocky outcroppings. Spur trails lead to headlands, the most rewarding being Eagle Point, with a view across the water to the city and Point Grey.

Immediately after this diversion, keep left on Arbutus Trail beside a twin-trunked cedar and left again to join Valley Trail on its way to the lighthouse. A short distance beyond this junction, a steep path descends to Starboat Cove, one of several delightful picnic spots around the southern tip of the peninsula.

Continuing westward, past the buildings, you will soon find yourself on a rock overlooking the lighthouse. A plaque gives details of its century-old history. Stay with the signposted Shore Pine Trail through the maze of paths on this side of the park, but don't pass up a side trip onto Shore Pine Point to look down along the rocky coast and across to Bowen Island.

From there, Shore Pine Trail takes you northward through stands of old-growth trees and the site of a blowdown to a junction with Seven Sisters Trail and Juniper Loop. Here, if your urge for exploration is still not satisfied, you could add Juniper Point to your bag of headlands by turning left. Otherwise, save that jaunt for another day and follow the gravel path out to the parking lot.

KILLARNEY LAKE

Round trip 8 km (5 miles) FAMILY HIKE
Allow 3 hours **EASY**
Good all year

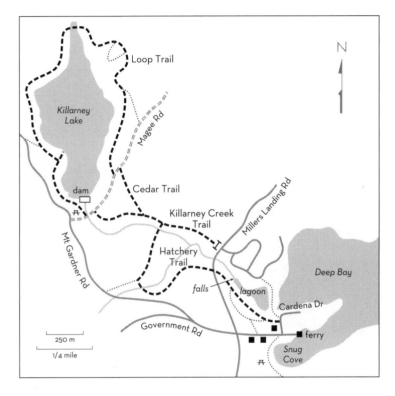

ENHANCED BY A short ferry ride from Horseshoe Bay, Crippen Regional Park on Bowen Island offers activities to suit the whole family: A stroll through the village of Snug Cove or along the causeway by the lagoon, a picnic by the harbour, a brisk climb to Dorman Point or the circular walk including Killarney Lake described here. Information about Crippen Regional Park is available at the library (once the Union Steamship Company Store) on Government Road.

> GETTING THERE You won't need your car on the island. Just drive Highway 1/99 to Horseshoe Bay in West Vancouver and leave your car in the pay parking lot. Ferries run almost hourly to Snug Cove on Bowen Island; phone B.C. Ferries at 1-888-223-3779 or go to their website at bcferries.com for sailing times and current passenger fares.

To reach Horseshoe Bay ferry terminal by public transit, take the Horseshoe Bay Express bus #257 from Vancouver or the #250 bus from Park Royal. For up-to-date information, contact TransLink at 604-953-3333 or visit their website at translink.ca.

> THE TRAIL For a clockwise circuit of the park trails and lake, walk north along Cardena Drive for about 100 m (110 yards) and turn left at the signpost to Killarney Lake. Two side trips present themselves as you set out on this trail. First, a diversion into Memorial Gardens offers a view from a rocky bluff overlooking Deep Bay to the mountains on the mainland. Farther along on the main trail, you can take a short path down to Killarney Creek falls and fish ladder.

Next, cross Miller Road and follow Hatchery Trail to Terminal Creek Meadows, passing on your way the fire-blackened remains of two giant cedar snags beside the trail. Go right on Meadow Trail, past the equestrian ring, and after crossing the creek, turn left onto Killarney Creek Trail. Keep left at the next fork, left again on Magee Road and follow signs to the lakeside picnic area.

To circumnavigate the lake, follow the west-side trail past a small beach to round the marshy end of the lake on long boardwalks. At the lake's northern tip, a bench invites you to sit and view the drowned forest across the tangle of shrubs and cattails.

The undulating trail along the east side of the lake provides views across the water to Mount Gardner. Stay right at an unmarked fork, crossing a bridge immediately after, and follow Killarney Loop Trail to its junction with Magee Road. Here, you must walk left for a few metres to find Cedar Trail entering the woods on the opposite side. Go straight ahead when you meet Killarney Creek Trail, this time following it to its end at a gate on Millers Landing Road. A right turn here will take you back to the falls above the lagoon, from where you can retrace your steps to the ferry slip or the blandishments of Snug Cove.

FOUR LAKES TRAIL

Round trip 6 km (3³⁄₄ miles)
Allow 2¹⁄₂ hours
Best April to November
Campgrounds at Alice Lake

Wheelchair accessible Campground
trails and Alice Lake Loop Trail
FAMILY HIKE
EASY

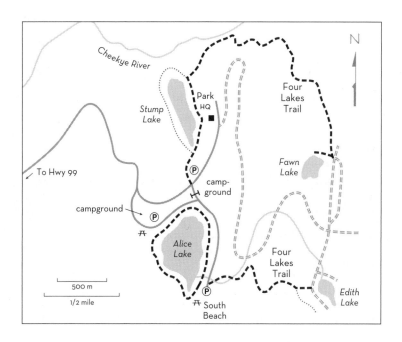

IF YOU WANT an easy, uncomplicated walk for the whole family
to enhance a picnic or camping trip in Alice Lake Provincial Park,
try this well-marked circuit. June is a good time to see Labrador tea
in bloom at Fawn Lake and twinflower, bunchberry and queen cup
in flower along the trail. Marsh buckbean grows in the water at the
edge of Stump Lake, and by June, the logs offshore have become
floating gardens bedecked with shrubs and flowers.

> GETTING THERE Drive north on Highway 99 for about 10 km
(6 miles) beyond the Squamish turnoff to a right turn signposted

to Alice Lake Provincial Park. At the park entrance, keep straight ahead toward the beach and picnic area. Drive to the far end of the parking lots and turn right on the road to South Beach parking and picnic areas.

> **THE TRAIL** Near the entrance to the South Beach parking lot you'll see a trail ascending beside a creek. This is your starting point for a circuit of the four lakes. After a short climb through the woods, you emerge into a more open area, soon to encounter a sign directing you left to Edith Lake.

To continue the circuit, walk north on the access road and keep left where the road forks at the end of the lake. After a further few minutes, where your route intersects a former logging road, follow signs for Stump and Fawn Lakes. In due course, you'll see a signposted path to Fawn Lake on your left. Be sure to take the side trip to this charming lake before going on with the circuit.

To proceed to Stump Lake, return to the signpost and take the trail up through the trees. Walking is pleasant and easy as the trail winds through shady woods toward the Cheekye River (this Squamish First Nation name means "fast-flowing water"). In about 15 minutes, follow the Stump Lake sign right, taking time, where the trail curves close to the river, to scramble down to the boulder-strewn beach for a view of the mountains to the west.

At the next T-junction, where Stump Lake can be seen through the trees, turn left to walk along the east shore of the lake—a delightful stretch with side paths down to the water. Take the left fork at the end of the lake and you will soon step out onto the main park road. Cross this and proceed southward past the campgrounds. The south beach parking lot can be reached by following the road or by taking the trail along the east or west shore of Alice Lake.

SKYLINE-COPPERBUSH CIRCUIT

Round trip 8 km (5 miles)
High point 400 m (1400 feet)
Elevation gain 300 m
(1000 feet)

Allow 3½ hours
Best April to November
MODERATELY EASY

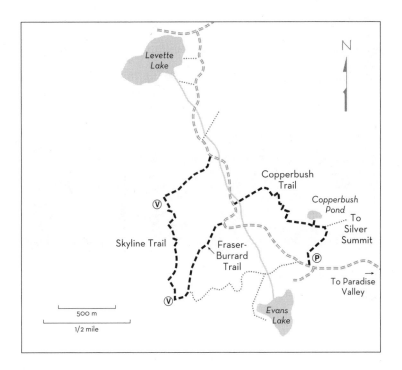

A TRAIL SYSTEM in the Evans Lake area offers some interesting low-level walking in the country between the Cheakamus and Squamish Rivers. Although the route stays below 500 m (1640 feet), views of the nearby Tantalus Range give an illusion of being high in the mountains. Spring is a good time for this hike, when the peaks are still snow-capped and the woods are coming alive. A visit to

View of the Tantalus Range

Levette Lake can easily be incorporated into the circuit, but in this case, allow 4½ hours for the entire walk.

> **GETTING THERE** From the Alice Lake junction north of Squamish on Highway 99, turn left toward Cheekye on the Squamish Valley Road. Immediately after crossing the Cheakamus River, bear right and follow Paradise Valley Road for 2 km (1¼ miles) to a left turn to Evans Lake, opposite the North Vancouver Outdoor School. Follow this rough road uphill for about 1.3 km (¾ mile) and park at a fork, where the private road descends left to the forestry camp at Evans Lake.

> THE TRAIL Since trails in the immediate vicinity of the Evans Lake camp are not open to the public, hikers following the clockwise circuit suggested here must start by tramping up the logging road toward Levette Lake. (The rough track ascending from the parking space is your return route.) After climbing for about 15 minutes, passing a 1-km marker and crossing a bridge, watch for the Fraser-Burrard Trail branching left from a bend in the road. This is your route to Skyline Ridge.

Fifteen minutes of climbing up the stony track brings you to a forestry sign and map, opposite which a trail (now closed to the public) descends to Evans Lake. Continuing ahead for a few metres, you'll find the road dwindles to a narrow path that climbs steeply to a ridge overlooking the Squamish River Valley.

Regrettably, the fast-growing conifers have reduced once-panoramic views of the Tantalus Mountains to tantalizing glimpses. Still, several bluffs invite you to pause as you follow the red markers along the salal-engulfed ridge path. After a steep descent, at the bottom of which a tree-trunk ladder helps the hiker across a tangled hollow, followed by a stiff little climb, you emerge onto a rocky summit. Two clearings open out, both satisfactory picnic spots with striking views of the Tantalus peaks.

The trail now descends steeply to meet the logging road at a bridge. Go left here if you want to visit Levette Lake, thereby adding 3 km (2 miles) to your circuit. Otherwise, if you are content to wander homeward, walk down the road for five minutes to pick up the Copperbush Trail. Watch for the path on the left, usually marked by red ribbons, near a jumble of rusty cables at the roadside. You can, of course, return to your car by staying with the road, but you will miss a fair sampling of backcountry wilderness by doing so.

After crossing the roadside creek on a bridge, the trail climbs briefly to an open bluff. Thereafter, it winds its way, marked now by orange triangles, among boulders and rocky outcrops, until, after about a half hour's walking, you arrive at the more gentle surroundings of Copperbush Pond. From here, unless you opt to take a side trip to Silver Summit, a further 15 minutes downhill takes you back to your car at the Evans Lake fork.

BROHM LAKE FOREST

Round trip 7 km (4½ miles)   **Allow** 3½ hours
High point 350 m (1150 feet)   Best May to November
Elevation gain 150 m (500 feet)   **EASY**

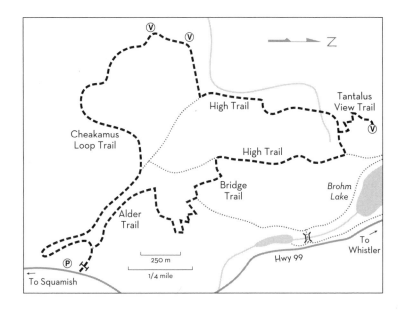

THIS CIRCULAR HIKE on B.C. Forest Service trails south of Brohm Lake offers great rewards for modest effort. On good-natured trails, through varied surroundings, you make your way to a succession of viewpoints facing the majestic Tantalus Range. Notable along the way are carpets of twinflower, adorned in early summer with exquisite pink blooms. Since even easy hikers need a challenge, that, too, is provided by a climb to a lookout for a breathtaking panorama. Choose a clear day.

> GETTING THERE To reach the forest trailhead, drive north from Squamish on Highway 99 for 2 km (1¼ miles) beyond the Alice

Lake turnoff and watch for a small parking area on the left, beside a yellow gate. If you are unable to make a left turn here, continue to the Brohm Lake parking lot, 2 km (1¼ miles) ahead, where you can turn around and drive back to the forest trailhead.

> THE TRAIL Walk up the old road, passing Alder Trail—your return route—and follow the forestry road around a hairpin bend for about 15 minutes to the start of Cheakamus Loop Trail, angling uphill to the left. After a brushy beginning, the trail soon opens out, bordered by sword fern and mats of twinflower, as it rises gently through mixed forest. After descending in the shadow of some towering rocks, you will see a side trail leading up to your first viewpoint, a rocky bluff with a splendid view of the Tantalus Range and Squamish Valley. A little way ahead, a second viewpoint, this one to the right of a bend in the trail, invites further dalliance.

Pressing on, however, toward the ultimate vantage ground, you descend past a jumble of rocks that have been split asunder by the forces of nature to join High Trail, on which you turn left. The Tantalus peaks remain visible as you continue northward, first through a clearing furnished with logging artifacts, later rising steadily toward a bulky rock eminence. By no means pass up the final assault on this daunting hump.

Turn left on Tantalus View Trail and persevere up the steep path, assisted now and then by giant stairs, until, after 10 or 20 minutes, you arrive, breathless, upon the summit. Wander over to the westfacing rocks, lean against a pine tree and gaze across the valley to the gleaming Tantalus icefields. The Cheakamus River is a greygreen ribbon below.

Eventually you must tear yourself away, descend the wooden staircases and continue on High Trail to the next junction. Leaving Brohm Lake for another day, stay right on High Trail until you come to the signpost for Bridge Trail. Go left on Bridge for a short distance, keeping an eye out for Alder Trail branching off to the right. This is your homeward stretch. After a gradual descent to the moister region of shrubs, ferns and vine maples, you step out onto the old road, only three minutes from the yellow gate and your car.

CAL-CHEAK TRAIL

Round trip 8 km (5 miles)   Campground at Cal-Cheak
Allow 3½ hours   **MODERATELY EASY**
Best May to October

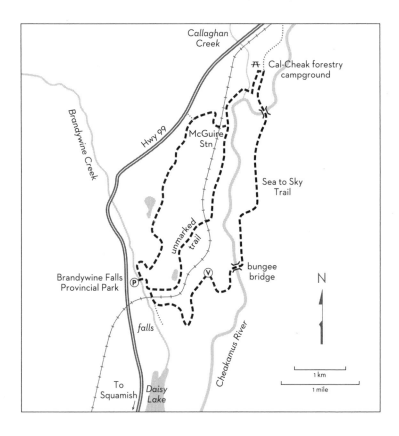

IF YOU ARE visiting Brandywine Falls Provincial Park, you could hardly miss the three separate signposts inviting you to hike up to the Cal-Cheak suspension bridge at the B.C. Forest Service Recreation Site. A circular trip is possible using the original hiking trail and the cross-country ski route, but today you also have the

Suspension bridge over Callaghan Creek

chance to sample a stretch of the newer Sea to Sky Trail. This ambitious project, similar to the Trans Canada Trail, is a point-to-point route for mountain bikers and hikers extending 180 km (112 miles) between Squamish and D'Arcy. Eventually, the trail is destined to link Horseshoe Bay with Lillooet.

The Brandywine to Cal-Cheak section of the Sea to Sky Trail is a remnant of a historic trail used by First Nations people and early pioneers travelling between Squamish and Pemberton. The terrain around Brandywine Provincial Park was formed eons ago by volcanoes and glaciers, leaving in their wake lava flows, basalt columns and the 70-m (230-foot) waterfall for which the park is named.

If you are camping at the B.C. Forest Service Recreation Site, you can of course reverse the route described, with Brandywine Falls as your destination and turnaround point.

> GETTING THERE Drive Highway 99 (Sea to Sky Highway) north from Squamish for about 37 km (23 miles) to the entrance to Brandywine Falls Provincial Park.

> THE TRAIL From the parking lot, cross the wooden bridge over Brandywine Creek and turn right on the main Falls Trail—left will

be your return route. Now you must make a decision. If you are keen to test your navigational skills, and footwork, on the original hikers' trail, turn left just before the railway track at the signpost reading "Unmarked Trail to Cal-Cheak Suspension Bridge." On this, you will scramble over lava rock and meander through lodgepole pine forest, all the while keeping an eye out for the occasional ribbons and markers. Once past the defunct McGuire Station, it is a short walk beside the turbulent Cheakamus River to its confluence with Callaghan Creek. Cross the suspension bridge to enter the Forest Service Recreation Site and find a table at which to rest or eat your lunch. When you're ready to leave, retrace your steps to the McGuire Station signpost to pick up your return route via the cross-country ski trail (see final paragraph).

If you opt to hike the Sea to Sky Trail to the Forest Service Recreation Site, continue along the main Falls Trail, cross the railway track and turn left at the signpost with the Sea to Sky logo, announcing "Cal-Cheak Suspension Bridge 4 km, Cheakamus Bungee Bridge 2.6 km." On this trail, which is graded and gravelled for bikes as well as hiking boots, you soon arrive at a viewpoint to Black Tusk and surrounding mountains, before pressing on to a crossing of the Cheakamus River at the famous bungee-jump bridge. On the east side of the river, the Sea to Sky Trail currently uses a forest service road, re-crossing the Cheakamus as it enters the recreation site. You'll discover that the campgrounds are divided into three separate areas; head for the southernmost campsite to find the way to the suspension bridge over Callaghan Creek. Cross the suspension bridge and walk downstream beside the Cheakamus River. After a stretch of open forest you'll arrive at what was once the McGuire whistle stop, from where you begin your return to Brandywine via the cross-country ski trail.

Cross the railway at McGuire and climb up to the service road. When you are within sight of Highway 99, go left through the gate onto the powerline right-of-way. After an open, undulating stretch, the trail passes through pine forest and some marshy areas before descending steeply beside Brandywine Creek to the wooden bridge and adjacent parking lot from where you began your journey.

CHEAKAMUS LAKE

Round trip 6 km (3³⁄4 miles)
or more
Allow 3 hours or more
Best June to October

Campgrounds at Cheakamus Lake
and Singing Creek
FAMILY HIKE
EASY

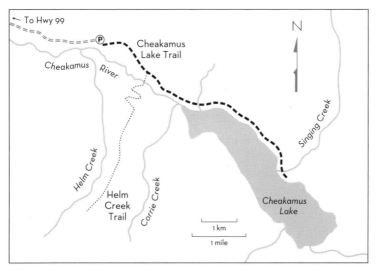

NESTLED AT THE foot of the Fitzsimmons Range, and just within
the boundary of Garibaldi Provincial Park, glacier-fed Cheakamus
Lake is ringed by peaks towering to 1600 m (5250 feet). The mostly
level trail and lakeshore campsites draw summer crowds of hikers,
fishers and mountain bikers. If you prefer tranquility and school
holidays are not a consideration, try to hike this trail in fall, when
peace enfolds the lake and the surrounding mountains await the
first snowfall.

> GETTING THERE Drive north from Squamish on Highway 99
(Sea to Sky Highway) for 50 km (31 miles) and turn right at the traf-
fic light (there is a B.C. Parks sign) onto Cheakamus Lake Road.
After about 400 m (440 yards), stay left on Cheakamus Lake Forest

Service Road (Eastside Main) and follow this gravel road for 7 km (4½ miles) to the parking area at the trailhead.

> THE TRAIL Stepping out eastward on the trail, accompanied by the roar of the Cheakamus River below, you are soon treading the forest path through groves of majestic amabilis and Douglas-firs. After about 30 minutes, you will reach a junction with Helm Creek Trail, a connecting route to Black Tusk and the high meadows, beginning from a crossing of the Cheakamus River. If you decide to take a side trip to see the crossing, allow a half hour and remember you will have to climb back up the steep trail.

Staying with the gentler Cheakamus Trail, you pass next through a damp area much favoured by devil's club, then through stands of hemlock and cedar, to emerge at the lake's outlet. The turquoise water with its mountain backdrop is arrayed before you. Having accomplished 3 km (2 miles), this may be as far as you choose to go for a family picnic.

For those with the time and inclination, the trail continues on the north side of the lake for a further 4 km (2½ miles), crossing many a stream and avalanche path. As you pick your way across rock slides bright with tiger lilies, paintbrush, valerian, mats of pentemon and stonecrop, you may see or hear pikas as they go about the business of harvesting grass and flowers in readiness for winter.

The view unfolds as you walk—to the east Overlord Mountain dominates the scene, then the McBride Range, with Mount Davidson, Castle Towers Mountain and the Cheakamus Glacier to the south.

You may not wish to go as far as the wilderness campsite at Singing Creek, 7 km (4½ miles) from your starting point, but there are many delightful spots and beaches along the way to serve as a destination before retracing your steps.

JOFFRE LAKES

Round trip 11 km (7 miles)
High point 1600 m (5250 feet)
Elevation gain 360 m
(1200 feet)

Allow 6 hours
Best July to October
MODERATELY DIFFICULT

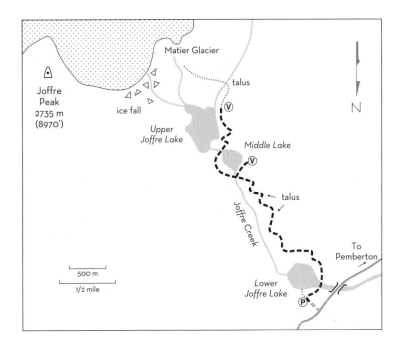

IF YOU ARE staying at Whistler, assign a clear day to the hike
to Upper Joffre Lake at the foot of the Matier Glacier. The 5-km
(3-mile) trail is more challenging than the statistics suggest, with
much talus to negotiate and repeated crossings of Joffre Creek in its
tempestuous fall from the icefields, but three turquoise lakes and a
close-up view of the glacier more than make up for the hazards of
getting there. Boots are essential and a walking stick is a help. You
will appreciate binoculars, too, for examining the ice formations.

Matier Glacier

> **GETTING THERE** From Whistler, drive north on Highway 99, taking the right fork at Pemberton, toward Lillooet. In the village of Mount Currie, turn right onto Duffey Lake Road, noting your odometer reading at this point. After leaving Lillooet Lake, the road climbs in a series of zigzags up the valley of Joffre Creek. About 23 km (14 miles) from Mount Currie, and soon after the bridge over Joffre Creek, watch for the parking area for Joffre Lakes Provincial Park on your right.

> **THE TRAIL** The first of the three lakes on your route is reached in a few minutes. Follow the Joffre Alpine Trail through the woods to the marshy outlet of Lower Joffre Lake. As you tread the boardwalks, look up to the left for a sight of the glacier, backed by Mount Matier and Joffre Peak.

After crossing the creek, the trail climbs gently on the west side of the lake. Glimpses of the sparkling green water are left behind as you veer away from the creek and rise higher up the side of the valley on a rocky, rooty path. After a half hour's climbing, you will encounter an extensive rockfall, after which the trail returns, briefly, to the creek, only to climb relentlessly away again. Glance upstream for an awe-inspiring view of Joffre Creek in its wild descent.

Depending on your pace over the rugged terrain, in about two hours' walking from the start, you will descend at last to Middle Lake. Before crossing the outlet creek, walk a short way along the side trail to the right for an unforgettable view of this gemlike body of water in its forest setting, dominated by the gleaming icefields to the south.

The walk along the lake's east shore ends all too soon, with the multiple crossings of the creek's many channels where it pours into the lake. Log bridges are provided, some narrow and slippery, requiring steps of catlike precision as you cross the tumbling water.

These obstacles overcome, you face the last steep ascent to timberline. After leaving the creek, the trail climbs alongside a dry gulch before levelling off as it approaches Upper Joffre Lake.

A path to the left leads down to the water, but the upper trail above the lake's western shore has its rewards too. Some open picnic spots present themselves as you near the south end of the lake, where you can sit and gaze across the water to the cliffs and glaciers, perhaps witnessing a block of ice weakened by the midday sun breaking away to thunder down toward the lake.

The trail continues beyond the end of the lake, rising over talus to a boulder pile close to the snout of the glacier, but this excursion is best left to experienced climbers. Unassuming hikers can rest in the sun before tackling the rough descent.

PITT RIVER GREENWAY

Round trip 8 km (5 miles)   FAMILY HIKE
Allow 2½ hours   **EASY**
Good all year

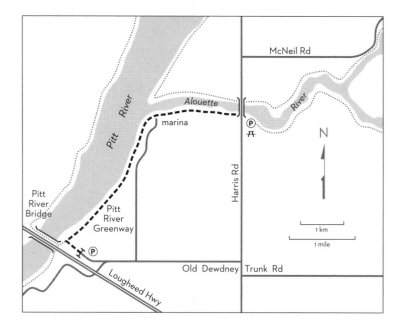

PART OF A network being created throughout the Lower Mainland, the Pitt River Regional Greenway uses existing dykes along the
Fraser, Pitt and Alouette Rivers. Future plans may see an unbroken
greenway continuing for 30 km (19 miles) to Grant Narrows at Pitt
Lake. The existing 20-km (12½-mile) stretch from the trailhead at
the south foot of Harris Road to its abrupt end at the Sheridan Hill
quarry is more than most walkers would want to tackle. We suggest
a more modest sampling. This section beside the Pitt and Alouette
Rivers offers water and mountain views, a lively marina and a riverside picnic area—leaving plenty more to explore on future outings.

Pitt Meadows marina

> **GETTING THERE** Turn left (north) off Highway 7 (Lougheed Highway) at the first traffic light east of the Pitt River Bridge, onto Old Dewdney Trunk Road. Immediately turn left again onto a short dead-end road and park on the shoulder before the vehicle barrier.

This starting point can be reached by public transit. Take bus #701 from Coquitlam Station, alight at Old Dewdney Trunk Road and Lougheed Highway and walk to the starting point. For up-to-date information, contact TransLink at 604-953-3333 or visit their website at translink.ca.

> **THE TRAIL** Walk down the road beyond the barrier, staying right where the cycle paths diverge, and go through the gate onto the dyke. Now you can put away your navigational skills and take pleasure in a straightforward stretch of the Pitt River Greenway.

As you leave the fringe of trees behind, the panorama unfolds. The wide tidal river sweeps past on your left, eager to unite with the Fraser. Tugs and pleasure craft go to and fro on the water; geese stake their claim to the marshes along the shore. To the northwest is the long line of Burke Ridge, with the knolls and marshes of Minnekhada Park below. North and east are the mountains surrounding Pitt Lake and the polder. Blueberry and cranberry bushes occupy the fields inland. Benches along the way invite a pause for contemplation.

As you approach Pitt Meadows marina at the mouth of the Alouette River, you'll find a different scene. In summer, this is a busy place where boats are unloaded from trailers and made ready for a day on the water. On a winter walk, the marina may be deserted, save for the ancient vessels and houseboats moored along the opposite shore and perhaps a family of swans feeding on seed left for them on the edge of the dock.

Heading upstream now beside the Alouette River, you will in due course spot the Harris Road Bridge ahead, presaging your destination and turnaround point. When you arrive at the bridge, cross Harris Road and enter the parking area opposite. Here you will find a Trans Canada Trail Pavilion, an outhouse or two and picnic tables on the riverbank. On a sunny weekend, hikers, joggers, cyclists and picnickers converge on this spot to avail themselves of the dyke paths along both arms of the Alouette. You could venture farther before retracing your steps to the Pitt River Bridge or start from here next time and explore more Alouette River dykes.

PITT RIVER AND MARSH

Round trip 9.6 km (6 miles)   **Wheelchair accessible** Pitt Lake
Allow 3½ hours   Dyke only
Good all year   FAMILY HIKE
                                    EASY

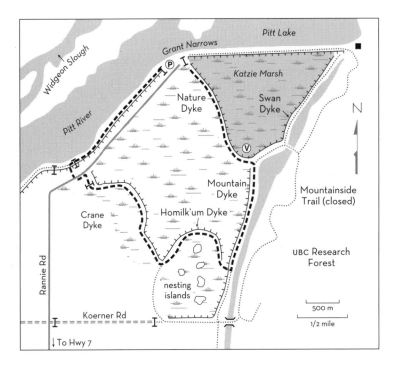

THE DYKES and marshland south of Pitt Lake are popular with hikers year round—as a winter walking ground, as a bird-watching spot during spring and fall and as a place for lazy walks along the dykes amid the tall grasses of summer. The polder is a haven for ducks, geese, herons, sandhill cranes and a variety of songbirds. Ospreys, hawks and eagles hold their place in the life of the marsh; beaver and muskrat busily burrow away at the dykes. Be sure to take binoculars.

Regrettably, the interesting mountainside trail bordering the eastern edge of the marsh is currently closed due to lack of maintenance, so for the time being, hiking is restricted to the network of dyke paths around the marshes. The fairly long circuit suggested here should satisfy most walkers in terms of interest and exercise. Please note: Crane Dyke is usually closed from mid-March to mid-July to preserve the peace and sanity of sandhill cranes during their nesting season. During this period, a shorter circuit using Nature Dyke, Swan Dyke and Pitt Lake Dyke can be substituted (refer to the map) and offers two observation towers from which to view the lake and marsh.

> **GETTING THERE** Pitt Lake is reached from Highway 7 by turning left on Old Dewdney Trunk Road, just east of the Pitt River Bridge. Turn left again on Harris Road, right on McNeil and left on Rannie Road to its end at Grant Narrows.

> **THE TRAIL** For the longer hike, pass through the gate onto the riverbank above the parking lot, turn your back on the lake and follow Pitt River downstream. In winter, you might see llamas being exercised on this dyke. After walking for about 40 minutes, you'll reach a gate and a track leading to Rannie Road. Walk left (north) on the road for a short distance to find the gate onto Crane Dyke on your right.

This wide, open dyke curves in a southeasterly direction, affording you a view of the mountains in the UBC Malcolm Knapp Research Forest. Turn left when you meet the dyke bordering Homilk'um Marsh. Continuing east on Homilk'um Dyke, then north onto Mountain Dyke, the full panorama of the mountains encircling Pitt Lake unfolds before you. Also visible is one of the viewing platforms on the lamented Mountainside Trail.

Your next objective is an observation tower, reached by turning left at the next junction. After a breather, continue past the tower onto Nature Dyke, a narrow path fringed by shrubs and cottonwoods, between Pitt and Katzie Marshes. Eventually, the facilities of Grant Narrows are glimpsed through the trees and your polder ramble is complete.

UBC MALCOLM KNAPP RESEARCH FOREST

Round trip 8 km (5 miles)   **Allow** 3½ hours

High point 340 m (1100 feet)   Good most of the year

Elevation gain 290 m (950 feet)   **MODERATELY EASY**

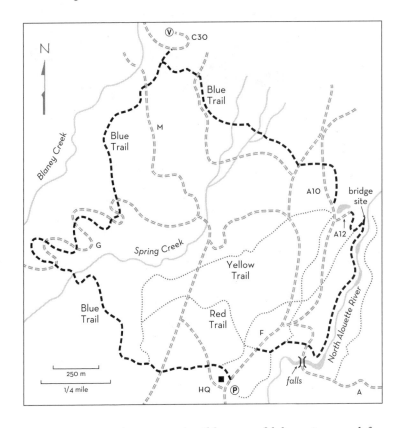

THIS 5000-HA (12,355-acre) wilderness of lakes, rivers and forested slopes is managed by the University of British Columbia for research and instruction in the practice of forestry. Information on the region's history and present use can be obtained from the forest headquarters.

Arboretum at forest headquarters

In the demonstration area at the forest's southern end, visitors can choose from four colour-coded trails, ranging from easy, well-groomed paths to a three-hour hiking trail. If this sounds a little tame, don't be misled: the circuit described here combines the Blue, Green and connector trails to provide a varied journey with plenty of ups and downs. Marking is discreet, so be careful to stay on route.

> GETTING THERE To reach the research forest from Dewdney Trunk Road in Maple Ridge, drive north on 232nd Street. After about 3.5 km (2 miles), a right fork onto Silver Valley Road takes you to the forest entrance.

> THE TRAIL Begin the circuit by walking behind the forest headquarters, where the combined Red, Yellow and Blue trails head west across the arboretum before entering the forest. After crossing a road, follow the marked Blue Trail branching left.

A stretch of open forest ends in a clear-cut area with a wide view westward over the polder, the Pitt River beyond. Your Blue route then continues through forest to a crossing of Spring Creek. Shortly after this, follow the well-marked trail across a road—the first of several meetings with G Road as you roughly parallel its winding course before striking off northward to rise on the east side of Blaney Creek.

After crossing M Road and climbing briefly to a fork, you have the option of a side trip. The left-hand trail rises to a road (C30), on which you turn right and ascend steeply for about 10 minutes to a viewpoint and mountain shelter. As well as a sweeping view of the Fraser Valley and Golden Ears, to the north you may glimpse the pointed building that houses the revolutionary liquid mirror telescope.

Retracing your steps to the fork, continue eastward on the Blue Trail—rough in places as it skirts a clear-cut area. After crossing two roads, you step out onto A10 Road near a small pond. Here is where you switch your allegiance from Blue.

It would be a pity to forgo a delightful stretch beside the North Alouette River, so take the spur road A12 heading sharp left just past the pond. In a short distance, take the unmarked trail descending on the right toward the river. Turn left when you meet the Green Trail and proceed to the site of the now-dismantled Mills Bridge, where you will spot another unmarked trail that meanders downstream. Ignore a trail branching right, and follow the riverside path to a shelter near the lower bridge and falls.

Having gazed at the falls from the bridge deck, it only remains to tramp up the road, turning left when you meet F Road, and walk the final 200 m (220 yards) to the entrance gate, having sampled a slice of a working research forest.

EAST CANYON TRAIL

Round trip 9 km (5½ miles)
High point 335 m (1100 feet)
Elevation gain 180 m (600 feet)
Allow 3½ hours

Best March to December
Campgrounds at Gold Creek and
Alouette Lake
MODERATELY EASY

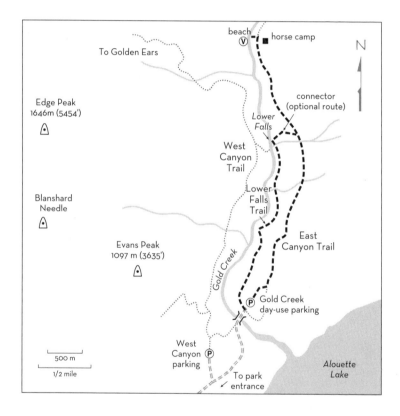

THE GOLDEN EARS massif for which this provincial park is named is tantalizingly out of reach for the day hiker, or indeed for any but the experienced climber. Less ambitious hikers, however, may venture by park trails into the upper Gold Creek Valley and thus get a taste of the rugged backcountry. One such trail traverses

Lower Falls

the forested slopes on the east side of Gold Creek, descending to an idyllic beach with a spectacular view of the peaks. East Canyon Trail, once a logging road and stony in places, is wide enough to accommodate hikers, equestrians and cyclists. An option for hikers who can cope with some rougher terrain is to combine the East Canyon route with Lower Falls Trail by means of a casual connector. A circular trip is always satisfying, especially when it adds one of the region's most beautiful waterfalls to the day's delights.

> **GETTING THERE** From Dewdney Trunk Road in Maple Ridge, follow the signs to Golden Ears Park via 232nd Street and Fern Crescent. Continue for about 14 km (9 miles) beyond the park entrance to the Gold Creek day-use area.

> **THE TRAIL** Walk north through the parking lots to find the start of Corral Trail heading off to the right from the hitching rack. Keep left at the first fork and go left again when you meet East Canyon Trail. Now you are properly on your way, rising gently through dense forest on a wide, sand-covered road pocked by horses' hooves. On

either side, mute stumps bear witness to a 1920s logging operation; massive boulders tell of ice-age upheaval eons ago.

Several creeks, or dry creek beds depending on the season, are crossed along the way. At one of them, perhaps a half hour's walking from the start, an old metal gate straddles the road. Farther ahead, you cross a creek on two giant logs, and a short distance beyond this logging relic, you may notice a trail heading left, currently marked by a red metal marker. This is the optional return route for the adventurous.

Continuing northward, you soon reach the highest point of the hike, where a break in the trees reveals the needlelike summit of Blanshard Peak across the valley. Descend now to river level and walk on until you come to a trail junction at the 4.58-km marker. To the right is a horse camp; the trail to the left leads to your turn-around point at a wide pebble beach. Edge Peak and the Golden Ears tower majestically over the scene. This is a fine place to picnic, dip a toe in the creek, study the ramparts or just while away some time before retracing your steps along East Canyon Trail.

If you decide to tackle the optional route to Lower Falls, watch for the beginning of the trail just past the 3-km marker. Be prepared for some steep sections as the path works its way through a blowdown area. Although rough, the trail is well used and marked by occasional B.C. Parks signs. Take it slowly and after about 15 minutes you will arrive safely at a fenced viewpoint above the falls. White water cascades down a staircase of rock into a deep green pool, then slides over the edge into a second thunderous fall.

Follow the trail down to a lower viewpoint and catch some spray before heading back to the day-use parking area along Lower Falls Trail—an easy 45-minute walk, with the creek for company.

KANAKA CREEK

Round trip 4 km (2½ miles)   FAMILY HIKE
Allow 2 hours or more   **EASY**
Good all year

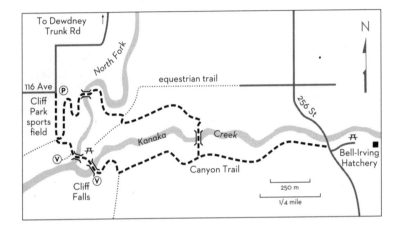

ON THIS SHORT up-and-down hike you'll follow a lively creek as it winds through mixed woodland and tumbles through sandstone canyons on its way to join the Fraser River. Kanaka Creek is named for early Hawaiian settlers, "kanaka" being the word for "person" in the Polynesian language. Employed on the Hudson's Bay Company ships in the late 1800s, many islanders stayed around Fort Langley, married Sto:lo Natives and bought themselves land across the river.

Although Kanaka Creek Regional Park comprises 400 ha (960 acres) and stretches 11 km (7 miles) upstream from the Fraser, access is at present limited to the trails described here and a separate section along the riverfront, reached from the Lougheed Highway east of its junction with the Haney Bypass. Future plans include trails linking the estuary to Cliff Falls and beyond to Kanaka Creek's headwaters on Blue Mountain. Today, your turnaround point is the Bell-Irving Hatchery, where chum and coho salmon fry are raised and released each spring to begin their seaward journey.

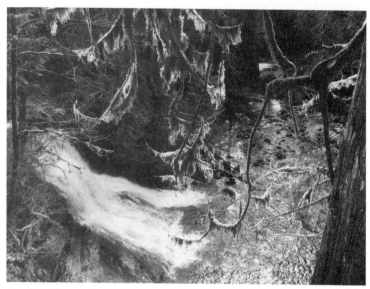
North Fork waterfall

> GETTING THERE From Maple Ridge centre, drive east on Dewdney
  Trunk Road for about 5.5 km (3½ miles) and turn right on 252nd
  Street. Follow this road around two bends to Cliff Community Park
  and leave your car in the parking lot beside the sports field.

> THE TRAIL Walk to the bottom of the sports field and descend
  through the woods to a bridge over the North Fork tributary. A short
  path to the right just before the bridge goes to a viewpoint overlooking a waterfall above the confluence with Kanaka Creek. Cross the
  bridge to enter Cliff Falls picnic area, situated between the creek's
  two separate arms. Go down to the viewpoint at the bottom of
  the grassy slope to see the water dance over the sandstone ledges.
  Upstream, as you cross the bridge over the main arm of Kanaka
  Creek, you'll see (if the flow is not too tumultuous) that the rock is
  pitted with potholes and saucers caused by boulders being ground
  into the soft sandstone over the ages.

  Continuing along the east side of the creek, you quickly come to
  the beginning of Canyon Trail, along which you head left. The path
  undulates through woods awash with dainty foamflower in spring

and summer. After passing between the cut sections of a giant dead-fall, you climb to a stand of tall hemlocks and cedars. Take note of the trail descending left—this will be your return route. For now, continue on Canyon Trail for a further 800 m (½ mile) until you step out onto 256th Street, almost opposite the entrance to the Bell-Irving Hatchery.

Walk up the drive to find the picnic area beside the creek, afterwards taking time to visit the rearing ponds and troughs. If you are there in spring, you might witness the release of smolts, during which some channels are drained, leaving resident crayfish exposed in the mud. The hatchery is open for guided tours most weekends between 1 and 3 PM.

Retrace your route to the trail noted earlier and descend to a metal bridge over Kanaka Creek. The beach below is a good place to look for fossils compressed in the slaty rock and to admire the maidenhair fern clothing the canyon walls. After a short climb from the bridge, the trail levels off to continue through alder woods. Follow signs for the North Fork Loop Trail, first to the right, then left on an equestrian trail that descends to yet another bridge across the North Fork. When you intersect your outward route, a right turn and a short climb take you back beside the sports field to your car.

HAYWARD LAKE

Round trip, Railway Trail 11 km (7 miles)
Allow up to 4 hours
Round trip, Reservoir Trail up to 20 km (12½ miles)

Allow 4 hours or more
Good all year
Campground at nearby Rolley Lake
FAMILY HIKE (west side)
MODERATELY EASY

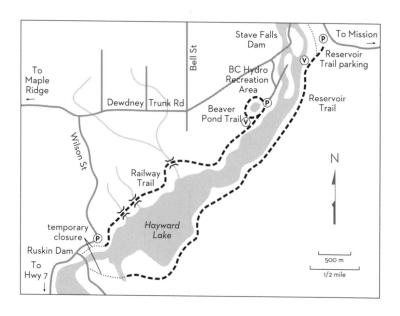

IN THE EARLY 1990S, two dams and a powerhouse were built at Stave Falls. With the completion of the Ruskin Dam downstream, Hayward Lake reservoir was formed. Later, B.C. Hydro developed the reservoir lands for recreation. As well as a picnic area, 16 km (10 miles) of trails were built to circumnavigate the lake. Today, seismic upgrading of the dams—a project that may last until 2018—has necessitated temporary closures that prohibit a complete circuit of the lake. The B.C. Hydro Recreation Area at the northern end of the lake will remain open throughout the project, though the beach may be closed when the water level is low. The west-side Railway

Trail will remain open between the recreation area and an upper (interim) parking lot on Wilson Street. Reservoir Trail on the east side will remain open from the parking lot on Dewdney Trunk Road, east of Blind Slough Dam, to the floating bridge on Hairsine Inlet. Both these trails are well worth hiking, even without the road links at Ruskin and Stave Falls Dams. We have described them separately. Please observe all posted signs. For up-to-date information on the seismic upgrading project, visit the website at bchydro.com/energy_in_bc/projects/ruskin_dam_powerhouse_upgrade.

Families with small children might prefer to park at the B.C. Hydro Recreation Area and content themselves with a short nature walk around a beaver pond and some of the gentle Railway Trail or tour the powerhouse at Stave Falls, where a visitor centre offers historical displays, a theatre and a gift shop. For details, contact B.C. Hydro at 604-462-1222 or visit their website at bchydro.com/stave_falls.

> **GETTING THERE** From the Pitt River Bridge on Highway 7 drive 6 km (3¾ miles) to a left turn onto Dewdney Trunk Road. (Don't take Old Dewdney Trunk Road immediately east of the bridge.) Drive a further 23 km (14 miles) east on Dewdney Trunk toward Stave Falls. Just before the dam, take the signposted B.C. Hydro Recreation Area access road downhill to the right. Those wishing to sample the longer and more challenging east-side trail should continue on Dewdney Trunk to the Reservoir Trail parking lot east of Blind Slough Dam. (Pedestrian access from the recreation area to the Reservoir Trail is currently restricted to weekends.)

> **RAILWAY TRAIL** The trail begins gently, following the bed of a long-gone railway built to carry supplies between Ruskin and Stave Falls. After passing the first of several old trestles, you climb away from the shore to cross several ravines on footbridges. Loop trails, provided with benches for catching your breath, allow you to explore the steep, forested slope. When you arrive at the upper parking lot, you must turn around and retrace your steps to the recreation area.

> **RESERVOIR TRAIL** A short distance from the parking lot, stay left where a trail branches right toward the dams. After crossing Brown

and Steelhead Creeks, you will see a signposted trail to Steelhead Falls; don't pass this up. In spring especially, these sparkling cascades tumbling through the forest are worth the short side trip. Back on route, you walk through second-growth forest of cedar and Douglas-fir on a trail constructed jointly by B.C. Hydro, the District of Mission and Forest Renewal B.C. The many hand-hewn seats along the way attest to the ingenuity of the trail builders and are welcome besides, as you tramp the ups and downs.

About two hours of walking will bring you to a lakeside spot with a long, welcoming bench. Bearing in mind that you must ultimately retrace your steps to the trailhead, this might be a reasonable turn-around point—until such time as a complete circuit of Hayward Lake Reservoir is again possible.

ROLLEY FALLS AND LAKE

Round trip 5 km (3 miles)

Allow 2 hours

Good most of the year

Campgrounds at Rolley Lake

FAMILY HIKE

EASY

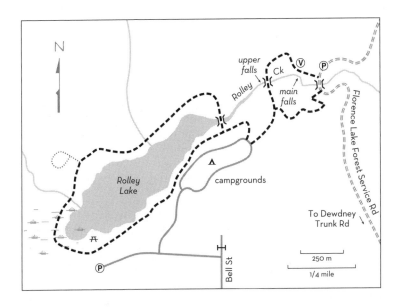

TUCKED AWAY ON a plateau above the dams on Stave Lake, modest, unruffled Rolley Lake has much to offer an outdoor-loving family: spacious campsites, a swimming beach and picnic area and a well-kept path around the lake. For those who prefer fishing to walking, small craft (but not motors) are allowed, and the lake is stocked with rainbow trout. Birds love Rolley Lake too. Woodpeckers and Steller's jays announce themselves; ospreys sail above the water; raiding parties of bushtits dart among the evergreen boughs. Most importantly, the bona fide hiking family can include the Rolley Falls Loop Trail in their itinerary, thereby adding waterfalls, views and exercise to the pleasures of the lake. Please note that Rolley Lake Provincial Park may be closed between October and April.

> GETTING THERE Unless you are already camping at the lake, a good way to make the most of this provincial park is to approach the Falls Trail from the Rolley Creek Bridge on the Florence Lake Forest Service Road. Drive east from Maple Ridge on Dewdney Trunk Road toward the Stave dams. Passing the sign to Rolley Lake at Bell Street, continue on Dewdney Trunk for a further 2 km (1¼ miles) to where the forest road heads left (north) immediately before the dam. Drive 2.5 km (1½ miles) to the small parking area by the bridge at Rolley Creek.

> THE TRAIL You will see the red markers of the Falls Loop Trail at both north and south ends of the bridge. Start from the north end, climbing the narrow path with the creek to your left. In a few minutes, after crossing a minor stream, you will come to a viewing platform below the falls—a splendid sight as the water plunges down its narrow canyon. The round, black hole at the base of the falls is an old mine shaft. As you walk on, a view of Stave Lake opens out below. After passing through a cleared area supporting a thicket of berry bushes, you will arrive at a bridge over the upper falls where a swift, but orderly, cascade drops from a broad ledge.

A short distance beyond the bridge you will notice the Falls Loop Trail—your return route—descending left to the road. But there is still the lake to explore, so on you go through the tall trees and beds of brilliant mosses to emerge onto pavement at the end of the provincial park campgrounds. Turn to the right and immediately right again on the marked trail heading back into the woods. This soon becomes a wide gravel path, leading to a bridge over the lake's outlet, which you cross to begin a counter-clockwise circuit of the lake.

A gentle 20-minute walk along the northern shore brings you to a bridge over an inlet stream, after which you pass through a glade of cedars before embarking on a long boardwalk across the marshy end of the lake. The day-use picnic area and beach lie just ahead.

To complete your circular walk, simply continue on the wide lakeshore path, ignoring connecting trails from the campgrounds, until you arrive back at the outlet bridge. Retrace your steps on the Falls Trail, but this time take the right arm of the loop to descend on the south side of Rolley Creek, enjoying the sound and sight of the falls again before you step out near your car at the bridge.

HICKS LAKE

Harrison, Fraser Valley north

Round trip 6.5 km (4 miles)
Allow 3 hours
Good most of the year

Campgrounds at Hicks Lake
FAMILY HIKE
EASY

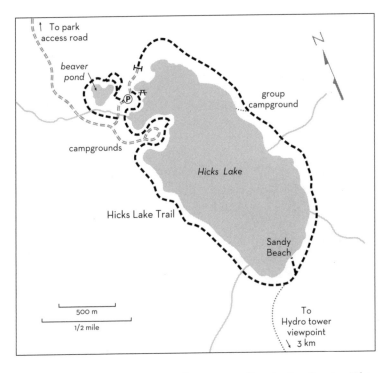

HICKS LAKE: A plain name for an appealing body of water. This popular lake in Sasquatch Provincial Park exudes a friendly atmosphere, with well-appointed campsites, canoe rentals, swimming beaches and a grassy picnic area sloping down to the shore. As well as the trail around the lake, a shorter path circles a beaver pond near the day-use parking area. While Hicks Lake is surely the perfect place for a family outing, vigorous hikers can add distance and elevation to the walk described by following an old logging road at the south end of the lake to a viewpoint on a hydro right-of-way. This side trip adds 6 km (3¾ miles) and 160 m (525 feet) of elevation to the lake trail.

> GETTING THERE To reach Sasquatch Provincial Park from Harrison Hot Springs, drive along Lillooet Avenue then north on Rockwell Drive past the marinas on the east side of Harrison Lake to a marked right turn immediately before the sign to Green Point. Take the right fork for Hicks Lake and stay left for the day-use parking areas.

> THE TRAIL For a counter-clockwise circuit, head for the picnic tables, beyond which a trail follows the lakeshore, crossing a dam at the lake's outlet to continue around the edge of the campground peninsula. As you enter the next bay, a Hicks Lake Trail sign sets you on your way along the forested western shore.

Up and down you go, through moist patches, then among massive cedar stumps, until at the end of the lake you meet an old road. Stay left here—right takes you on the side trip mentioned earlier, with its view of Seabird Island and the Fraser Valley—and in a few minutes you will spot a path leading down to the water. Known as Sandy Beach, this is a good place to sit on a log and rest, or eat your lunch, with the lake stretching before you.

The old road, now softening into trail and bordered by ferns and wildflowers, makes an easy return along the east side of the lake. Not long after passing the entrance to the group campsite you will arrive at a yellow gate, beyond which are the parking lots. But don't forget the beaver pond; to add this to your itinerary, walk down the road for a few metres and you'll spot the Beaver Pond Loop sign on your right. In fact, there are two loops, the right-hand path being a short, woodsy walk joining the main loop at a viewing platform overlooking a beaver lodge. Keep right to complete the loop around the pond and you will soon find yourself back beside the road not far from your car, or your campsite.

DEAS ISLAND

Round trip 6.5 km (4 miles),
or 8 km (5 miles) with Island
Tip Trail
Allow 2 hours
Good all year

Wheelchair accessible The
park access road to the
sheltered picnic area
FAMILY HIKE
EASY

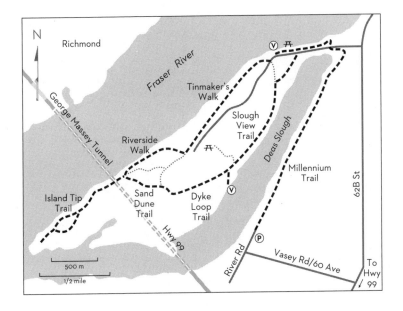

ON THIS ISLAND that is no longer an island, being linked by a causeway to the mainland, you'll walk through woodland, meadows and dunes, beside a sheltered slough and along the banks of the Fraser River, with its busy traffic of tugs, barges and freighters. This much-loved regional park boasts a sheltered picnic area as well as riverside tables.

Deas Island was named after its first settler, tinsmith John Sullivan Deas, who in 1873 built and operated a cannery here. Although nothing remains of this enterprise, three restored buildings have

Eagles' nest

been moved to the island from their original sites in Delta, adding to the historical interest. Details are provided in the park leaflet, available from the kiosk opposite the Burrvilla residence.

A worthwhile addition to your exploration of the island is first to walk a stretch of Delta's Millennium Trail along the Deas Slough dyke, thus adding farm fields and buildings, and perhaps racing skiffs, to the sights of the day.

> **GETTING THERE** Leave Highway 99 at exit 28, south of the George Massey Tunnel. Follow the "River Road north" sign left (east) over the overpass and turn left at the traffic light onto 60th Avenue (Vasey Road). Turn right on River Road and park at its end, near the gate onto the dyke.

Although this starting point cannot be reached by public transit, you could take bus #640 from Scott Road Station and alight on River Road near the entrance to Deas Island Park to join the hiking route. For up-to-date information, contact TransLink at 604-953-3333 or visit their website at translink.ca.

Step out along the dyke beside the quiet waters of the slough, fields of crops inland. Once past the farm buildings, take the path left through the parking lot, crossing the park access road to walk along the riverbank. Seals and diving birds can often be seen offshore; resident eagles circle overhead. Opposite is the one-room Inverholme Schoolhouse, built in 1909.

After taking a look at Burrvilla and viewing the river from the observation platform, head west along Tinmaker's Walk. Keep an eye out for a large eagles' nest high in a cottonwood tree to the left of the path. In spring and summer, songbirds busy themselves in the thickets alongside the trail. Stay right on Riverside Walk.

When you join Island Tip Trail, decide whether to begin your return trip by turning left on the signposted Sand Dune Trail or add a further 1.6 km (1 mile) to your walk by continuing to the south-western tip of the island. For this, you stay straight ahead, passing over the tunnel access and hiking past a channel marker to a beach. Beyond this point, the trail is informal and often wet in winter and at high tides. If you persevere to the extreme tip of the island, you'll look across the mouth of Deas Slough and its marina, Ladner Marsh and Kirkland Island beyond. The trail loops back to re-cross the tunnel.

Heading homeward on Sand Dune Trail, you pass first through a stand of shore pine and an army of horsetail plants. Keep right on Dyke Loop Trail. After taking the short side trip on the right to a viewpoint over Deas Slough, continue on the sandy Slough View Trail (the path to the left goes to a picnic area) as it opens out into Fisher's Field.

As you near the buildings, take Tidal Pond Trail to the right, crossing the bridge over the pond and following the trail out to the park access road. From here it only remains to retrace your steps past the rowing club to Millennium Trail and tramp the dyke path back to your starting point.

BRUNSWICK POINT

Round trip 6.5 km (4 miles)
or more
Allow 2½ hours
Good all year

Wheelchair accessible dyke path
from the end of River Road
EASY

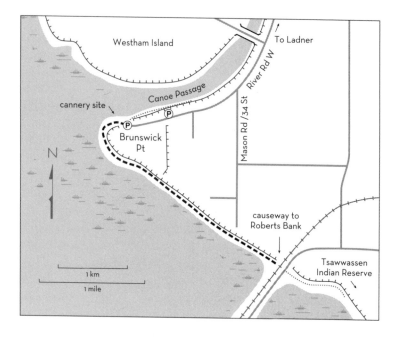

WHEN TRAILS ARE icebound, a brisk walk is still possible along the countrified stretch of dyke around Brunswick Point at the mouth of the Fraser's south arm. This tidal marsh, not far from the George C. Reifel Migratory Bird Sanctuary, attracts a variety of winter migrants, and the bay itself can be a fascinating sight when frozen into humps and ridges. Take binoculars.

> GETTING THERE From Highway 99 south of the George Massey Tunnel, take Highway 17 (Victoria Ferry) exit 28. Drive south for

1.6 km (1 mile) to the intersection with Ladner Trunk Road. Turn right here and continue west into Ladner, jog half-left onto 47A Avenue, which in turn becomes River Road West. Follow River Road past the turnoff and bridge to Westham Island. If you wish to include a short stretch along the river, there is limited roadside parking and access to the dyke opposite the flat-roofed house protected by a row of poplars. Otherwise, continue to the road's end at the gate.

> THE TRAIL Put on your hat and gloves, climb up onto the dyke and set off west along Canoe Passage. Approaching Brunswick Point, you will see rows of pilings—all that remains of one of the oldest salmon canneries on the river.

As you turn south, there is brackish tidal marsh, growing rushes, cattails and various sedges on the seaward side and agricultural land on your left. Groups of swans and snow geese can often be seen at the edge of the open water or flying to and from Westham Island. Herons and marsh hawks hunt along the fields and ditches; red-winged blackbirds call from the cattails. A few metres beyond the second pair of benches, paths lead to a sheltered picnic table below the dyke. Nearby is an outhouse whose now missing door once boasted the legend "Taj Mahal."

If you choose to walk farther along the dyke, Roberts Bank Superport dominates the scene. The twin terminals contribute to the economy by exporting millions of tons of coal each year and provide a foothold for the giant cranes of Deltaport container facility. Before reaching the causeway, you might find a comfortable piece of driftwood on which to rest, while watching mallards, grebes and sandpipers feeding at the water's edge. Your return walk is enhanced by the view of the mountains to the north.

55

BOUNDARY BAY DYKE

Round trip (south section)
10 km (6 miles)
Allow 3 hours
Good all year

Wheelchair accessible 12th Avenue
dyke and viewing platform
FAMILY HIKE
EASY

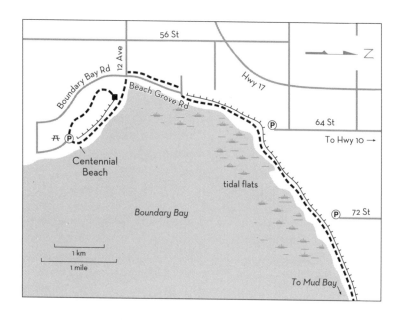

BOUNDARY BAY IS bordered by true salt marsh, the beds of
eelgrass and other marine vegetation providing a feeding ground
for vast numbers of migratory waterfowl and shorebirds. Keen bird
watchers should make this a winter trip to see the greatest variety
of birds; others may enjoy the beaches in summer or simply a brisk
walk along the open dyke.

Since the dyke path around the bay extends for 16 km (10 miles),
which is more than most walkers would want to tackle at one time,
we have described it in two sections. Families may find the southern

Bald eagle

walk, including Boundary Bay Regional Park and Centennial Beach, the more interesting for children.

> **GETTING THERE** From Highway 99, south of the George Massey Tunnel, take Highway 17 (Victoria Ferry) exit 28. Follow Highway 17 for 1.6 km (1 mile) and turn left (east) at its intersection with Ladner Trunk Road (Highway 10). Turn south on 64th Street and drive to its end at the dyke.

Although this starting point cannot be reached by public transit, you could take the #601 bus from Bridgeport Station to 12th Avenue and Boundary Bay Road and join the hiking route at midpoint. For up-to-date information, contact TransLink at 604-953-3333 or visit their website at translink.ca.

> **THE TRAIL** Setting off southwest along the dyke, toward Beach Grove and Point Roberts, look to both right and left for birdlife. Eagles, hawks and herons hunt over the fields as well as the shore.

The dyke ends at Beach Grove. It is better now to take the right-hand footpath and walk for 15 minutes along quiet Beach Grove

Road than struggle through the swampy stretch of beach below the houses. You rejoin the dyke at 12th Avenue for the final leg through Boundary Bay Park.

Through the gate, the dyke heads first east, alongside tidal flats harbouring hundreds of ducks and shorebirds, then south among the dunes. In spring, flocks of black brant geese sojourn here to feed on their migratory journey north. Centennial Beach, your turn-around point, offers driftwood, picnic tables, a playground and other facilities, as well as a view of Mount Baker on the eastern horizon.

It is possible to use an interesting inland return route to the dyke gate at Beach Grove. To locate this, cross the parking lot to its north-west corner and follow the foot trail beside a drainage ditch—a fishing ground much favoured by herons. Thereafter, keep to the left generally until you spot a path to a pumphouse beside the main dyke, where a bridge enables you to cross the ditch and rejoin your outward route.

If you elect to hike the northern section of the dyke, that is, east-ward toward Mud Bay, it should be noted that parking is allowed at the ends of 64th and 72nd Streets and at Delta Heritage Airpark (104th Street) only.

Throughout fall and winter, immense flocks of dunlin feed along the mudflats on this side of the bay, and you may be fortu-nate enough to witness the breathtaking aerial ballet they perform to escape a marauding falcon. White undersides flashing in the sun, the flock soars and swoops in disciplined formation, presenting no easy target for the predator. Snowy owls are occasional winter visitors to this area and may be spotted resting on driftwood along the shore.

East of 112th Street, Boundary Bay dyke path meets up with the western end of Surrey's Mud Bay Park, offering a further 2 to 3 km (1 to 2 miles) of path and shoreline trail to explore.

56

Surrey

TYNEHEAD REGIONAL PARK

Round trip 5.6 km (3½ miles)
Allow 2 hours
Good all year

Wheelchair accessible Salmon
Habitat Loop and Perimeter Trail
FAMILY HIKE
EASY

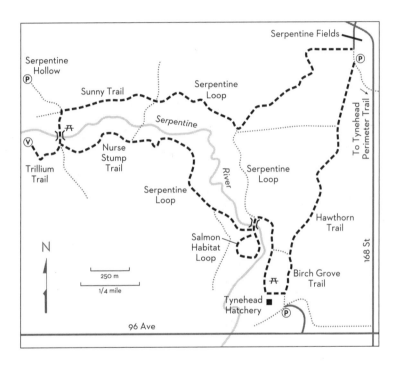

THIS TUCKED-AWAY PARK in Surrey is surprisingly peaceful considering its proximity to a Highway 1 interchange. Five km (3 miles) of trail loop around the headwaters of the Serpentine River as it winds through forest and farmland on a 27-km (17-mile) journey to Mud Bay. The area was logged in the 1880s, leaving many large stumps and nurse logs among the second-growth cedars and vine maples. Birds and small mammals find a safe haven here.

A fish hatchery, run by the Serpentine Enhancement Society, is situated at the southern edge of the park. Hatchery-raised coho, chum and chinook salmon are released in the spring to return, according to their appointed life cycle, to spawn in the Serpentine's secluded waters. Children will enjoy climbing to the viewing platform at Serpentine Hollow and following a salmon's life story on the Salmon Habitat Loop. They might even spot a troll or two in the forest.

These are trails you can enjoy in any season. They are graced with woodland flowers on a spring hike, shady on a hot summer's day and sheltering on a rainy one.

> GETTING THERE To make the most of the trail system, a good place to start is the Serpentine Fields entrance on 168th Street. Leave Highway 1 at exit 53 and drive south on 176th Street (Pacific Highway). Turn right (west) on 96th Avenue and right again on 168th Street for a further kilometre. The parking area is on the left, just before a bend.

Although this starting point cannot be reached by public transit, you could take bus #388 from 22nd Street Station, alight at 168th and 96th Avenue and walk to the Tynehead Hatchery to join the hiking route. For up-to-date information, contact TransLink at 604-953-3333 or visit their website at translink.ca.

> THE TRAIL Start by taking the trail from the northwest corner of the parking lot. Stately broadleaf maples stand guard over this remnant of old farmland. Turn right when you reach the Serpentine Loop Trail. After encountering a number of bridges spanning feeder streams and passing some massive cedar stumps with century-old springboard notches, you will arrive at a junction. Take the right-hand trail (ignore the trail heading north to 164th Street) as it breaks out into open meadow before re-entering the forest and crossing several more streams on its way to the Serpentine Hollow picnic area. One of the park's largest trees, a Sitka spruce, stands beside this stretch of trail.

From the top of the steps, walk left to the grassy clearing with its shady picnic tables. In summer, you might want to visit the butterfly garden before crossing the river. From the far side of the bridge, head right to climb Trillium Trail for a bird's-eye view from the tree-hugging platform.

To continue, stay south of the river and follow it downstream on Nurse Stump Trail, later rejoining Serpentine Loop Trail. Before re-crossing the river on an arching bridge, you could add the interpretative Salmon Habitat Loop to your itinerary. Afterwards, turn right at the end of the bridge to reach the Tynehead Hatchery and picnic area. If the hatchery is open, volunteers are usually willing to answer questions and show visitors around.

For the next leg of your trip, follow the signposted Birch Grove Trail from the southeast corner of the picnic area; by branching off it to the right on Hawthorn Trail, you can return across open mead-owland (a dog off-leash area) to the Serpentine Fields entrance and your car.

But your ramble need not be over yet. Those looking for a longer hike can include the more recently developed eastern section of the park. Tynehead Perimeter Trail is a blacktopped multi-use pathway linked to the pedestrian/cyclist overpass spanning Highway 1, all part of a network of Surrey greenways. To embark on this addition, follow the multi-use path from the parking lot, cross 168th Street and keep going. The circular path is 4.8 km (3 miles) long, with some gentle ups and downs. Although different in character from the western trails, the route is furnished with occasional sculptures and informative, often whimsical, exhibits. Don't miss the list of "Dos and Don'ts for Voles"!

57

Surrey

SEMIAHMOO RAMBLE

One-way trip 8 km (5 miles)
Allow 3 hours or more
Good all year

Wheelchair accessible Trails at
Elgin Flats
FAMILY HIKE (Elgin Heritage Park)
EASY

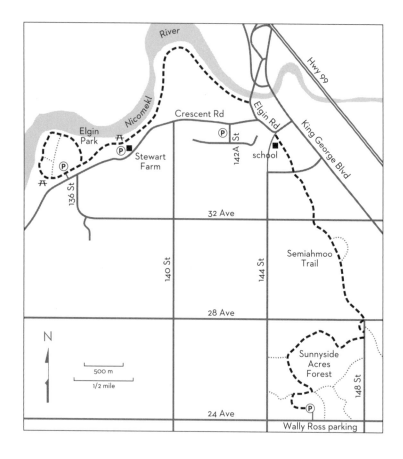

THIS WALK COMBINING three of South Surrey's treasures ideally requires the use of two cars. If a second vehicle is not available, you could devise a partial route for a there-and-back walk. Some possible parking places are shown on the map. Or you could arrange your outing to take advantage of public transit (see Getting There).

For a one-way trip, your starting point is Sunnyside Acres Urban Forest—a haven for birds, small mammals, coyotes and black-tailed deer—followed by a section of the Semiahmoo Trail. Once a route used by Native peoples and early settlers for transporting goods between the Fraser River and Blaine, the Semiahmoo Trail fell into disuse after the arrival of the railway. Today, surviving fragments have been preserved by Friends of Semiahmoo Trail and are maintained by community members.

From the bridge on Elgin Road, a newer pathway along the Nicomekl River skirts a golf course before arriving at the Stewart Farm in the heart of Elgin Heritage Park. Built by John Stewart in 1894, the Victorian farmhouse was home to the Stewarts for more than 50 years, during which the family helped to establish the community of Elgin by building the river dykes, school and community hall. The restored farmhouse is now a living museum, open to visitors most days, and hosts a number of events throughout the year. A short walk beyond the farm and marina are Elgin tidal flats, whose fields and shoreline are inhabited by waterfowl, shorebirds, herons, owls and other raptors.

> GETTING THERE (FOR A TWO-CAR TRIP) Leave Highway 99 at exit 10 in Surrey and follow the signs for Crescent Beach. After passing 140th Street and the main entrance to Elgin Heritage Park and the Stewart Farm, continue to a second entrance farther west (a few metres past 136th Street) and leave one car in the Elgin Flats parking lot. Drive via 136th Street, 32nd Avenue and 144th Street to the Wally Ross parking area at Sunnyside Acres Urban Forest on 24th Avenue.

Although this starting point cannot be reached by public transit, from the end of your hike near Stewart Farm you might be able to board bus #352 (a peak-hours only service) as it travels west on Crescent Road. Alight at 148th Street and 24th Avenue and walk back to your car at Wally Ross parking lot. For up-to-date information, contact TransLink at 604-953-3333 or visit their website at translink.ca.

> THE TRAIL From the parking lot, keep right at the first junction and stay left on Alder-grove Trail until you come to a sign for Chickadee Loop. Here you turn sharp left to begin half a clockwise circuit of the forest. Stay faithfully with Chickadee Loop signs until you step out onto 148th Street. A short walk left brings you to the west end of a pedestrian overpass. Walk left down the ramp, cross 28th Avenue at the traffic lights and continue straight ahead on a paved section of the Semiahmoo Trail. Farther ahead, a path to the right leads to benches beside a catchment pond.

After crossing 32nd and 34th Avenues, the trail then passes beside Elgin School to emerge on 144th Street at the junction with Crescent Road. It is best to cross 144th Street and walk west along Crescent Road until you can see both ways before attempting to cross. On reaching the Esso station, turn right on Elgin Road and make your way to a stone cairn just before the bridge. After reading the history of the Semiahmoo Trail, you are ready to go left between the posts onto the Nicomekl dyke path. Look for an eagles' nest perched high above the houses.

As you follow the path around Nico-Wynd Golf Course, you have a fine view of the river, with its collection of moored vessels, splendid and otherwise. At low tide, you'll see herons hunting on the mudflats. Look out, too, for straying golf balls and obey the signs. When the Nico-Wynd works yard comes into sight, stay right past the information board. After skirting a tidal marsh, keep right where the trail forks and you will soon arrive at an open grassy space with an apple orchard on your left. Walk up the slope past a pole barn filled with old agricultural machinery to visit the Stewart farmhouse. Be sure to take a look inside if the house is open.

Afterwards, walk past the washroom building and the weaving shed to the lower parking lot and take the trail going west into the woods. Some grand old trees overlook this path; if you are there in early spring, carpets of snowdrops will take your breath away. Entering the tidal flats, turn right on a trail that follows the shoreline or branch off on paths that pass through the interior fields (look for an owl barn there) and cut across the cattail marsh on a boardwalk. Back at the parking area, your Semiahmoo Ramble is over. All that remains is to drive back to Sunnyside Forest for your other vehicle.

CAMPBELL VALLEY

Round trip 8 km (5 miles)
Allow 2½ hours
Good all year

Wheelchair accessible Little
River Loop Trail only
FAMILY HIKE
EASY

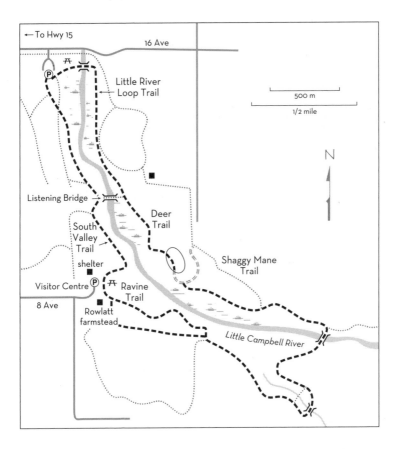

FOR A CHANGE of scene from mountain and forest, try this pas-
toral walk in Campbell Valley Regional Park, south of Langley. Suitable for an active family, the route suggested takes you from the

Rowlatt farmhouse

valley floor to open pasture, through woodland and creekside meadows. On the way, you visit the restored Annand/Rowlatt Farmstead, complete with old farm machinery and rebuilt barn. The park trails can be used all year, though in spring, quiet Little Campbell River sometimes floods the valley bottom, making the interesting boardwalk sections impassable. The region provides a habitat for deer, coyote, rabbits and owls, as well as waterfowl and songbirds.

> GETTING THERE From Vancouver, leave Highway 1 at exit 53 and drive south on 176th Street (Highway 15) to its intersection with 16th Avenue. Turn left (east) on 16th Avenue and proceed to the park's North Valley entrance, east of 200th Street.

> THE TRAIL From the information kiosk, look for a path to the left (east), named Little River Loop Trail on the park map, which takes you through lily-of-the-valley beds to cross the river on a long footbridge. Follow the trail upstream, beneath old cedars, for about 800 m (½ mile), as far as the sign to the Listening Bridge. After a side trip to the bridge for a close-up of wetland habitat, backtrack to

the east side of the river and follow the minor Deer Trail through a shrubby meadow. When you reach an oval track, known as Little River Bowl, walk to the right and leave the bowl on the old road heading right toward a clearing. Follow this road around the bend, watching for a narrow (possibly unmarked) path, still Deer Trail, entering the woods on your right.

The path meanders beneath tall birches and alder to a junction with the Shaggy Mane equestrian trail. Turn right here and right again to another bridge, on which you cross Little Campbell River to complete your circuit on the west side.

Stay on the main equestrian trail across some open marshland. After crossing a stream on the main bridge, the track veers northward across a meadow. In about 800 m (½ mile), just before a bend, take Ravine Trail descending through the trees on your right. Immediately after crossing a small creek, you may go left to visit the Annand/Rowlatt Farmstead or right to follow Ravine Trail through the forest. In the latter case, you will emerge at the bottom of a field below the farm to join a path running northward from the farm to a picnic area. From there, the South Valley (8th Avenue) visitor centre, garden and covered picnic shelter are nearby.

It is an easy half hour's walk to your car via the South Valley Trail descending east from the outdoor picnic tables. Having reached the bottom of the valley, stay on the west side of the river, passing through sheltered meadows and along a forest path, back to the north parking lot.

ALDERGROVE LAKE REGIONAL PARK

Round trip 6.5 km (4 miles)   FAMILY HIKE
Allow 2¹/₂ hours   **EASY**
Good all year

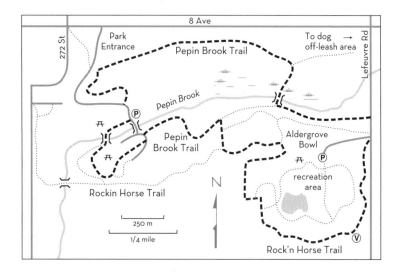

HERE'S A PLEASING family walk through woodland, meadow and berry fields, with a choice of picnic grounds.

Much of this park is a feat of reclamation. For years, this region has been scarred by the extraction of gravel, but abandoned workings are being transformed into lakes and ponds, and the area now supports a network of hiking and equestrian trails. If this sounds somewhat artificial, rest assured that the trails are countrified and peaceful, graced by wildflowers in season and alive with birdsong. The route suggested can easily be shortened or lengthened by referring to the map.

> GETTING THERE Although tucked away close to the Canada-U.S. border, the park is not difficult to find. Leave Highway 1 at exit 73, drive

Viewpoint bench

south on Highway 13 (264th Street) and turn left on 8th Avenue. Immediately after crossing 272nd Street, turn right at the Aldergrove Lake Regional Park sign and follow the access road to its end at the parking areas. Leave your car in the first parking lot, before crossing the bridge.

> THE TRAIL To begin this clockwise circuit, walk back on the road for a few metres to where the signposted Pepin Brook Trail heads north across a field. After a short climb beneath old broadleaf maples and Douglas-firs, the trail levels off to open out at the top of a grassy slope. The hut at the top of the hill houses a telescope used by the Royal Astronomical Society for searching the heavens.

Go right from the bottom of the field, making your way through the forest and crossing several creeks. Stay right where a trail leads to a dog off-leash area and descend to a marshy meadow and a bridge over Pepin Brook. Here you discover that the modest waterway sliding through the shrubs and sedges is home to an endangered ice-age survivor—the Salish sucker. (Look for a small greenish fish with a long snout.)

Turn left at the end of the bridge and make your way up to Lefeuvre Road. Walk right (south) on the road for a few metres, ignoring the gated access road, until you spot the signposted Rock'n Horse Trail entering the woods on your right. Follow it southward. Soon after passing another ice-age relic, known simply as Big Rock, you can pause at a viewpoint facing south and east across open farmland toward Mount Baker.

Next, Rock'n Horse Trail swings west then north, breaking into the open alongside berry fields, from where paths lead down to Aldergrove Bowl, with its picnic area, paths and man-made lake. After passing a bench overlooking the Bowl, turn left at the next junction. In less than 400 m (¼ mile), watch for a trail on the right signposted "To Pepin Brook." Follow this short path down through the woods, staying left to pass through a barrier for riders and turning left when you meet Pepin Brook Trail. The brook is glimpsed through the trees as you walk westward to emerge in the upper parking area. Picnic tables now occupy the site of what was once a popular man-made swimming pool for children.

When it's time to leave, cross the wooden footbridge west of the washrooms to return to your car.

DERBY REACH

Round trip 9 km (5½ miles)   Campground at Edgewater Bar

Allow 2½ hours   FAMILY HIKE

Good all year   **EASY**

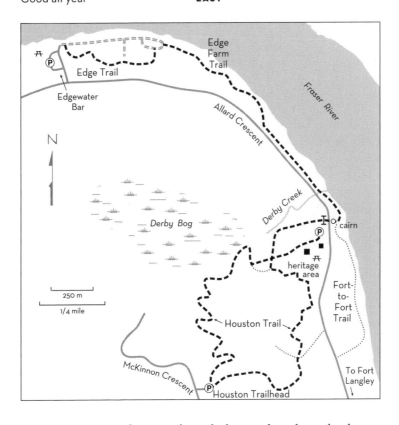

A WALK BESIDE the river, through the woods and over land once farmed by pioneers is yours to enjoy in Derby Reach Regional Park on the south side of the Fraser River. En route, you will stand on the bluff once occupied by the first Fort Langley and stroll by a farmhouse built in 1909 and a 130-year-old barn transported from Rosedale. Stout-hearted walkers can include some or all of the

Cairn at Derby Reach

Fort-to-Fort Trail (see Hike 61). Families with small children may prefer to make the picnic area at the heritage site their final destination for a round trip of 5 km (3 miles).

> GETTING THERE The best starting point for the hike described here is Edgewater Bar on Allard Crescent. Leave Highway 1 at exit 58,

go left (north) over the overpass and turn right on 88th Avenue, then left on 208th Street. Go right onto Allard Crescent and after about 2 km (1¼ miles) watch for the park entrance on the left.

> THE TRAIL From the information kiosk, walk through the campers' entrance to find the signposted Edge Trail heading into the trees on your right. The path winds through woodland dominated by giant cottonwoods to join the gravel campsite road at its end. Turn right here and right again through the gate onto Edge Farm Trail. After opening out into a meadow, the trail hugs the riverbank, presenting views of the foreshore log booms and Haney waterfront across the river.

Next, you tramp along a roadside stretch before crossing Derby Creek and climbing from river level to the historic site. Unless this is to be your turnaround point, the best plan is to save the sightseeing for your return and carry on now with the circular Houston Trail. To do this, cross the road opposite the cairn marking the site of the original fort and go through the gate opposite. A five-minute walk along this connector brings you to a bridge over a stream and a junction with the Houston Trail proper. Turn right to begin the circuit.

Now you need only follow the well-mannered path beneath stands of conifers and ancient broadleaf maples (side paths lead to the edge of Derby Bog), and after negotiating some small ravines, you will emerge at the equestrian unloading area—Houston Trailhead. You are halfway around the loop, so on you go, taking in your stride more ups and downs but soon rewarded by glimpses of the Fraser River and Fort-to-Fort Trail, before descending to the junction from which you began the circuit.

Here, if you wish, you may return to the heritage site by crossing the bridge and taking the path across the marshy field on your right. The path ascends to a grassy area surrounding the historic buildings— your chance to explore the site or rest at the orchard picnic tables before retracing your steps to Edgewater Bar. For variety, you could return to the parking lot via the campsite road instead of taking Edge Trail.

FORT-TO-FORT TRAIL

Round trip 8 km (5 miles)

Allow 2½ hours

Good all year

Campgrounds in Brae Island
Regional Park

FAMILY HIKE

EASY

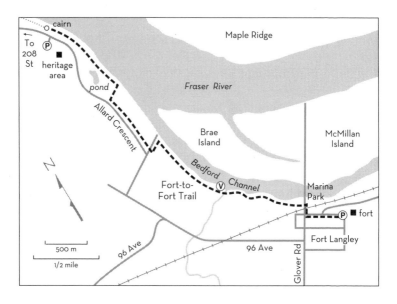

FOR AN EASY hike into British Columbia history, you could explore the Fort-to-Fort Trail connecting the site of the first Hudson's Bay Company fort, built in 1827 on the south bank of the Fraser River, with its later location 4 km (2½ miles) upstream, now a national historic site in Fort Langley village.

Taking almost 12 years from concept to completion, the riverside trail is now enjoyed by walkers, runners and cyclists. The route is well marked and supplied with benches and viewing platforms along its more picturesque stretches. Information panels at the Derby Reach Heritage Area describe the fort's history and life in the short-lived Derby townsite. Upstream, the village of Fort Langley offers

Canoe Club dock, Fort Langley

an abundance of museums, antique stores and tea shops, as well as the restored Hudson's Bay Company fur-trading post within its log palisade—a fitting destination for a historical journey.

> GETTING THERE To start from the Derby Reach Heritage Area, leave Highway 1 at exit 58, go left (north) over the overpass and turn right on 88th Avenue, then left on 208th Street. Go right onto Allard Crescent and drive for about 4 km (2½ miles) to the Heritage Area parking on the right.

Although this starting point cannot be reached by public transit, you could take bus #502 from King George Station to Langley Centre and bus #C62 to Fort Langley and reverse the hiking route. For up-to-date information, contact TransLink at 604-953-3333 or visit their website at translink.ca.

> THE TRAIL Having read the inscription on the roadside cairn marking the site of the first fort, look for the Fort-to-Fort sign, with

its fish-and-fort logo, and set off across the meadow to Derby Bluffs for views over the river to the northern mountains and eastward to Mount Baker.

The trail passes a pond and veers inland to continue beside Allard Crescent for a short distance before entering a wooded area. After crossing a creek and negotiating some minor ups and downs, you work your way back to the river, now facing the cottonwood-lined shores of McMillan Island across the Bedford Channel. Soon you will arrive at a viewing platform and pump station at the mouth of the Salmon River. Looking upstream, you can see the Jacob Haldi Bridge to McMillan Island. Closer at hand, you may spot a dozing heron or a kingfisher diving from the willows to try its luck in the Fraser's turbid water.

Leaving the pump station, take the signposted path to the left through the trees (trails to the right lead out to the road). The final stretch of trail skirts a residential area. Following the wide gravel path along the riverbank and past the rowing club dock, you will emerge beside the Fort Pub. Cross Glover Road and follow Fort-to-Fort signs into Marina Park. This is a good place to picnic, while imagining the steamboats unloading supplies destined to travel by canoe up the river's rapids and canyons to farther trading posts along the Fraser River. To complete the odyssey, walk up Church Street and turn left on Mavis Avenue to visit Fort Langley National Historic Site before retracing your steps to the site of the first Fort Langley.

MATSQUI TRAIL—WESTERN SECTION

Round trip 6 km (3¾ miles)   Campground at Mission
Allow 2 hours   Bridge Trailhead
Good all year   **EASY**

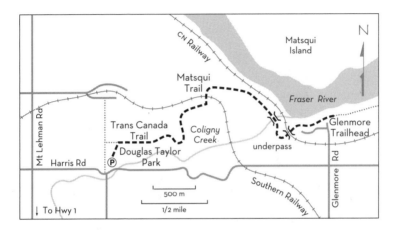

FIELD, FOREST, WETLAND and river are yours as you hike the western section of the Matsqui Trail. This entire trail along the south side of the Fraser River is a model of cooperation, comprising the Fraser Valley Regional Trail, 14 km (9 miles) of Trans Canada Trail, miles of dykes leased from the City of Abbotsford and passage, by agreement, through Matsqui First Nation lands.

Although the use of two cars is an ideal way to sample a long stretch of the Matsqui Trail, the undulating western end makes an interesting there-and-back hike on its own, with a satisfying turn-around point at the Glenmore Trailhead. This shared trail is popular with equestrians; give way to them and remember that horses are easily spooked by sudden sounds and movements. Also, please note that at spring run-off, the area around Coligny Creek may be flooded.

> GETTING THERE To reach your starting point at Douglas Taylor Park, leave Highway 1 at exit 83 and drive north on Mount Lehman Road. Turn right on Harris Road and in less than 1 km (½ mile) watch for a Trans Canada Trail sign indicating Douglas Taylor Park on the left.

> THE TRAIL Follow the path from the northeastern corner of the parking lot and turn right when you meet the Trans Canada Trail. Now you can march along, enjoying a view across the fields to Mount Robie Reid, wider mountain views unfolding as you walk.

Soon the trail descends into woodland dominated by huge fern-clad broadleaf maples. A short distance beyond the notice announcing your entry into Matsqui First Nation lands, you become aware of a railway on your left, and after passing through a ravine, you step over a low barrier to cross the railroad tracks. A further 10 minutes of walking brings you to a bend in the trail, beyond which you descend gently into wetland where cottonwoods tower above a tangle of salmonberry canes and skunk cabbage flourishes in damp hollows.

After crossing the bridge over Coligny Creek and rising to dyke level, you are confronted first by another railway, which you cross via an underpass, then by a gravel road. Follow the Trans Canada Trail signs across the road and you will soon emerge from the woods opposite a farm at the foot of Glenmore Road, your turnaround point only a few metres to the left.

From the open space beside the gate onto the dyke, you can look out across the river to Matsqui Island, upstream to Mission Bridge and to the mountains behind Mission. To the east, Matsqui Prairie stretches to the bulk of Sumas Mountain, and in the south, Mount Baker rises resplendent over the Fraser Valley.

You may, of course, continue eastward along the dyke as far as your legs will carry you—it's a further 3.3 km (2 miles) to the Mission Bridge Trailhead, with its riverside picnic grounds and other facilities—but many will be content to picnic or dally at Glenmore, watching river traffic and perhaps cedar waxwings feeding among the willows, before meandering back to Douglas Taylor Park.

CULTUS LAKE TRAILS

Round trip 11 km (7 miles)
High point 300 m (985 feet)
Elevation gain 260 m
(850 feet)
Allow 4½ hours

Good most of the year
Several campgrounds in the park,
including Entrance Bay
MODERATELY EASY

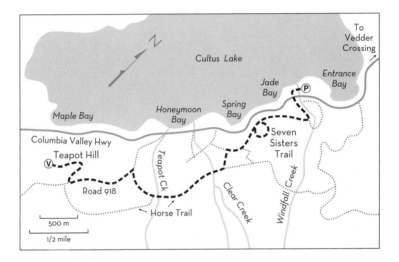

HIKERS LOOKING FOR a peaceful outing in the ever-popular
Cultus Lake Provincial Park should plan an off-season trip. In
spring, when wildflowers line the trails, or later, when leaves are
turning colour and campgrounds are deserted, tranquility prevails.
The route described offers a fair sampling of the park trails, linking
two short hikes with a stretch of the longer, more challenging equestrian trail. Quaintly named Teapot Hill provides a fitting climax,
with its vantage point overlooking the lake and neighbouring valley.

> GETTING THERE An easy way to reach the park is to leave High-
way 1 at exit 104, take No. 3 Road to Yarrow and follow the signs to
Cultus Lake. On Columbia Valley Road, drive past Cultus Lake village and park in the Entrance Bay day-use area.

Starflower

> **THE TRAIL** From the west end of the parking lot, cross the little bridge leading to the Jade Bay boat launch, walk to the left and cross the highway to enter the campgrounds opposite. Keeping to the right, walk uphill to find the signposted Seven Sisters Trail entering the woods just past campsite no. 7.

During spring and early summer, beds of starflower and vanilla leaf line this beautiful forested trail. After about 20 minutes of gentle climbing and descending, you will arrive at the grove of the Seven Sisters. By means of a long staircase, you may take a circular walk among these giant Douglas-firs, discovering as you go that some sisters, alas, have fallen.

The trail now continues toward Clear Creek. Ignore the first narrow trail ascending left, but as you approach the campgrounds, take the next, wider trail heading uphill to the left. This is your connector to the Horse Trail, upon which you will step out a few minutes later. Turn right, cross the creek and begin a steady half-hour climb through the woods.

After crossing Teapot Creek beside a picturesque broken bridge, you will reach a trail junction. For the shorter, less strenuous route to Teapot Hill, take the right-hand trail. Turn left when you reach the service road (Road 918) and proceed for about 300 m (330 yards) to where the Teapot Hill Trail branches right. (If you chose the longer route via the Horse Trail, you will meet Road 918 a few steps west of this point.)

On a track worn smooth by hundreds of feet seeking exercise, you climb to a bluff overlooking the lake. Nearby stands one of nature's wonders—a tall Douglas-fir scarred along its length by a lightning bolt. Having caught your breath, you are ready to tackle the final push to the summit. From that modest peak you may gaze west across the Columbia Valley to the international boundary and north to Vedder Mountain. Below lie Maple Bay and Lindell Beach, at the south end of the lake.

If you are daunted by the prospect of retracing your up-and-down journey, you could consider descending to the highway on the service road and making your way back to Entrance Bay by walking through the lakeside campgrounds. Beyond Spring Bay, though, you would need to walk on the highway shoulder for the remaining 400 m (¼ mile) to your transport.

VEDDER RIVER TRAIL

Round trip 9.4 km (6 miles)
Allow 3 hours
Good all year
Wheelchair accessible Much
of Vedder River Trail

Campgrounds at the end of
Giesbrecht Road, off Vedder
Mountain Road
FAMILY HIKE (Heron Reserve trails)
EASY

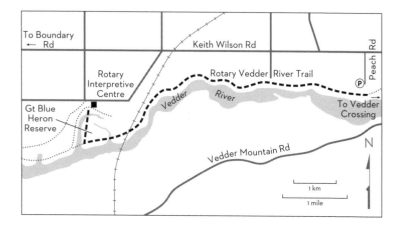

HERE IS A good way to combine part of the Rotary Vedder River Trail with a visit to the Great Blue Heron Nature Reserve. This admirable trail, now combined with the Trans Canada Trail, accompanies the river downstream from the bridge at Vedder Crossing to the point where the untamed water is harnessed into a canal. During spring run-off, the green and white water rushes by, swirling around sandbars piled high with debris.

The Heron Reserve, lying in the floodplain near the end of the river's free run, is home to one of the largest nesting colonies in the Lower Mainland. Trails loop around the lagoons; an observation tower provides an overview, with Cheam Peak resplendent to the east. An interpretive centre, funded and built by the Chilliwack Rotary Club and run by volunteers of the Great Blue Heron Nature

Rotary Centre, Great Blue Heron Reserve

Reserve Society, houses artifacts and displays, as well as televised films of life in the heronry taken by cameras perched high in the cottonwood trees. The centre is open daily from 10 AM until 4 PM and from 11 AM to 3 PM in the winter months. The reserve is open year round.

> **GETTING THERE** Leave Highway 1 at exit 104 and follow No. 3 Road east toward Yarrow. In slightly more than 3 km (2 miles), turn left on Boundary Road. Turn right to cross the Vedder Canal on Keith Wilson Road Bridge. Continue on that road for 6.5 km (4 miles), turn right on Peach Road and park at its end near the river.

> **THE TRAIL** Set off westward on the riverside trail, following Rotary/TCT signs. The path is popular but wide enough for walkers, joggers and cyclists to share without mishap. Benches along the way invite you to pause and watch mergansers navigating the swift current and anglers casting their lines from the sandbars. Nature lovers will find tansy, yarrow, pea vine, borage and chicory growing in

a glorious tangle beside the path. Inland, the minor waterways of Peach Ponds provide a safe haven for juvenile coho and steelhead.

After crossing a wooden bridge at a bend in the trail and passing beneath the railway, you'll come to a boulder-strewn beach opposite which an equestrian trail branches right into the woods. Take this path—it bypasses a stony section by the river and is soft underfoot as it winds beneath giant cottonwoods. After rejoining the main trail and crossing another bridge, you'll arrive at a gate and sign for the Great Blue Heron Nature Reserve. Turn right and follow the road to the Rotary Interpretive Centre; side trails lead to the shore of South Lagoon, from where you have a good view of the heronry across the water.

When you've rested or eaten your lunch at the picnic tables behind the centre, spend some time looking at the displays and talking to the volunteers on duty. Be sure to pick up a brochure. If time allows, explore the short Salwein Loop Trail. Or, if the Heron Colony Loop is open (it closes for nesting season between March and July), the trail on the west side of the lagoon will bring you back to the gate you passed through earlier—ready to return along the Vedder River Trail to Peach Road.

65

Galiano Island

BLUFFS PARK

Round trip 9.6 km (6 miles)   Campgrounds at Montague Harbour
Allow 4 to 5 hours   **EASY**
Good all year; May for
wildflowers

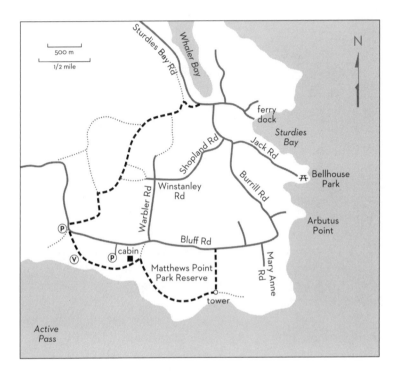

TO CONSIDER GALIANO Island as "around Vancouver" might seem a stretch, but this rewarding day trip is a favourite with mainland hiking groups.

Named after Spanish explorer Dionisio Galiano, this long, narrow island supports vegetation special to its dry climate. Stonecrop, spring gold and blue-eyed Mary hug the rocky bluffs; blue camas lilies cover the headland at Bellhouse Park; calypso orchids grow beside the forest paths. On the shore, strange sandstone formations

Sandstone formations

and tidal pools create a moonlike aspect. Ocean views are breathtaking; otters, seals and orcas are often spotted. Turkey vultures circle overhead.

On the walk between the ferry terminal at Sturdies Bay and Bluffs Park you'll take quiet country roads, a forest trail and a heavenly path along open, sunny bluffs, with a side trip to Bellhouse Provincial Park. Trails are plain to follow, though some are unmarked; read directions carefully.

If you have time while waiting for the ferry back to Tsawwassen, there are craft shops and studios to visit. Galiano never disappoints.

> GETTING THERE B.C. Ferries currently has two sailings a day from Tsawwassen to Sturdies Bay on Galiano Island. For details, consult a B.C. Ferries schedule or visit their website at bcferries.com. Leave Highway 99 at exit 28 in Delta and take Highway 17 to Tsawwassen ferry terminal. Leave your car in the (pay) parking lot and board as a foot passenger.

By public transit, take bus #620 from Bridgeport Station to Tsawwassen ferry terminal. For up-to-date information, contact TransLink at 604-953-3333 or visit their website at translink.ca.

> THE TRAIL From the ferry slip, walk up Sturdies Bay Road (noting Max and Moritz's food stand at the bottom of the ferry parking lot for when you come back). Don't turn left onto Burrill Road but continue straight ahead toward Whaler Bay, watching for a wooden archway and Sturdies Bay Trail sign on the left. Follow this for a minute or two until you see Bluffs Trail heading left into the woods. This is your route.

Ignore the first trail branching left and continue through the woods until you come to an unmarked fork. Go left and uphill here. Ignore two unmarked paths to the left and descend to a T-junction. Go left here and in a few minutes you'll step out onto a gravel road. Turn left again and, beside a vehicle turnaround at a bend in the road, you'll see two trails, one heading uphill and one descending to a gully. Take the uphill one and climb to the summit of Bluffs Park. This is a great place to have lunch, see the seals hauled out on the marker rock below and watch the ferries surging through Active Pass. Opposite is Helen Point on Mayne Island, and Navy Channel between Mayne and North Pender Island.

Meander east along the bluffs (wildflower book in hand perhaps), past a shelter and a parking area. After descending past an abandoned cabin, continue down the track to an unmarked trail on the right. Follow this through a jungle of broom to a hydro right-of-way on which you turn left for a few steps then almost immediately go right and uphill on another unmarked path into the woods. The path is plain to follow as it climbs then levels off to wander eastward beneath tall trees and through patches of broom, with occasional views over Active Pass. After descending past a sprawling lichen-clad Garry oak, you eventually arrive at a transmission tower. Here is where you leave the bluffs to return to civilization. Take the service road on the left and turn right when you meet Bluff Road. Tramp along it (it later becomes Burrill Road) for about 2 km (1¼ miles) as far as Jack Road.

To include Bellhouse Park in your itinerary, follow Jack Road and Bellhouse Road to the park entrance. A path rounds the headland. A picnic table on the open, rocky bluff is well placed to observe an eagles' nest opposite; in early spring, you might spot an eaglet flopping about in the nest, tended by its formidable parents. Walk down the slope to the beach.

If the tide is out and the rocks are dry, surefooted hikers who can cope with a scramble could consider walking back to Sturdies Bay along the beach. *Do not attempt to do this at high tide or if the rocks are wet and slippery.* Think about the ferry departure time, too. If you decide to go ahead, allow 45 minutes for this adventure and be aware that there is a tricky spot to negotiate where a creek runs down to the beach. Having overcome this obstacle, and perhaps having seen the river otters that favour this spot, continue past tidal pools and sandstone formations to where the driftwood ends and the beach takes a turn to the right. Locate and scramble over a concrete retaining wall in the hedge onto a narrow path leading up to a gate into the ferry parking lot.

If the beach is not accessible, then you must backtrack from Bell-house Park on Jack Road and return to Sturdies Bay along Burrill Road. Remember to get a boarding pass from the ticket kiosk in the parking lot before you walk down to the ferry slip for the voyage back to Tsawwassen.

66

Silver-Skagit, Hope

SKAGIT RIVER TRAIL

**Round trip upper or lower
section** up to 13 km (8 miles)
High point 600 m (2000 feet)
Elevation gain 100 m (350 feet)
Allow 4½ hours

Best June to October
Silvertip provincial campgrounds
near 26-Mile Bridge
MODERATELY EASY

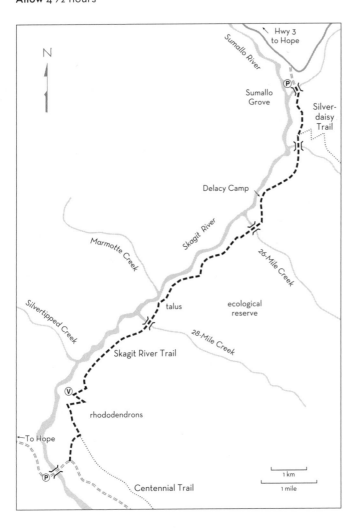

DESPITE ITS LENGTH, the mostly level trail along the east bank of the Skagit River, from its confluence with the Sumallo River to Silver Skagit Road, is perfect for the non-expert hiker. If you are staying in Hope, or camping in the area and can arrange for someone to drop you off at Sumallo Grove and pick you up on the Silver Skagit Road six hours later, that is ideal; otherwise, you must choose one end or the other for a there-and-back trip. For this reason, described here are the upper and lower sections as separate hikes, each about 13 km (8 miles) return and about 4½ hours long.

Originally known as the Whatcom Trail, constructed in 1858 to connect the United States with the brigade trails to the B.C. Interior, the route was later used by gold miners, immigrants and trappers. Today, it offers the hiker a sampling of impressive coastal forest, the company of a lively river and a variety of plants ranging from rhododendrons (mid-June is their flowering time) to lichens. Note, too, that bears are sometimes encountered on this trail.

> GETTING THERE—LOWER SECTION Leave Highway 1 at exit 168, west of Hope. Immediately before the bridge over Silverhope Creek, turn right (south) on Silver Skagit Road. Drive 43 km (27 miles) on the good gravel road to the Skagit River day-use parking area, located on the north side of 26-Mile Bridge. A few metres farther along the road, you will find the trailhead for Centennial and Skagit River Trails.

> THE TRAIL Continue along a leafy lane for about 15 minutes until you come to a parting of the ways. Here, Centennial Trail turns southeast toward the Chilliwack River Valley, and your Skagit River Trail heads in the opposite direction through stands of lodgepole pine with an undercover of rhododendron bushes.

Soon, a short climb to surmount a bluff is rewarded with a view through the trees of Silvertip Mountain opposite, its glacier gleaming below the peak. After this pause, you descend to the river, the milky-green water racing by as you walk along the bank beneath giant cottonwoods. Next, you must push your way through huckleberry and wild gooseberry bushes surrounding a flood area, then pass through a tract of deadfalls before coming to a log bridge spanning 28-Mile Creek.

You are now entering the Skagit River Cottonwoods Ecological Reserve, established to protect the magnificent black cottonwoods of the region, as well as western red cedars and Douglas-firs. The trail now rises and descends in a discouraging fashion. About 15 minutes after leaving 28-Mile Creek, you will traverse an open talus slope with a view across the valley toward Marmot Mountain; this might be a good lunch spot and turnaround point for the lower hike.

> GETTING THERE—UPPER SECTION For this expedition, drive east from Hope on Highways 5 and then 3, for 34 km (21 miles) to the picnic site at Sumallo Grove—a superb stand of virgin forest on the right side of the highway.

> THE TRAIL From the parking lot, follow the trail south to a footbridge over the Skagit River. There is a good view of Silverdaisy Mountain from midstream. In about 1.6 km (1 mile), you will pass the hiking trail to the mountain on your left and shortly afterwards cross Silverdaisy Creek. Moss and mushroom enthusiasts will find much to interest them at the foot of a talus slope reached a few minutes later.

Next is a descent amid huge Douglas-firs, followed by a half hour's walk downstream to a riverside glade known as Delacy Camp. You will notice how flood water has washed away the soil from the roots of the cedars along the bank.

After crossing 26-Mile Creek, the trail rises to negotiate steep bluffs before entering the ecological reserve. It is a 45-minute walk through the reserve, at which point you will have linked up with the lower hike from Silver Skagit Road. If that is not your goal, there are pleasant picnic spots to be found 800 m (½ mile) into the reserve, where the trail converges with the river.

You can make yourself comfortable on the pebbly beach and watch dippers feeding in the shallows or just gaze at the mountains opposite while the green water slides by.

HOPE-NICOLA VALLEY TRAIL

Round trip 10 km (6 miles)   **Allow** 3½ hours
High point 330 m (1100 feet)   Best April to October
Elevation gain 190 m (620 feet)   **MODERATELY EASY**

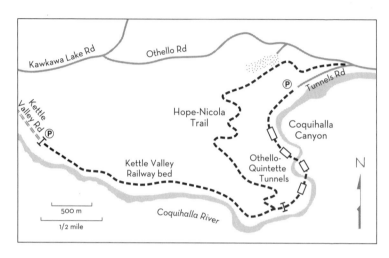

MANY VISITORS TO Hope walk through the Othello-Quintette Tunnels and take a stroll along the old Kettle Valley Railway bed. Those looking for a more challenging outing can include the Hope–Nicola Valley Trail, thereby sampling even more of the region's colourful history. This old cattle road, once used to transport supplies between the coast and the Princeton/Merritt areas, has been in place since the 1870s and is amazingly well preserved. Please note that the Coquihalla Canyon Recreation Area is closed from November to March. Note also that frequent rock slides in the canyon may block the south exit from the tunnels. Before embarking on the circuit described here, check with Hope Visitor Centre at 919 Water Avenue, telephone 604-869-2021 or visit the Coquihalla Canyon Provincial Park website for up-to-date information. In the event of a closure, a return trip from the Kettle Valley Road gate to the pass is still a worthwhile hike of about 6 km (3¾ miles).

> GETTING THERE From Hope, drive east on Kawkawa Lake Road. After crossing the Coquihalla River, turn right beside the cemetery onto Kettle Valley Road and park at its end near the gate.

> THE TRAIL Stepping out upstream along the old railway bed (now part of the Trans Canada Trail), you will have glimpses of the Coquihalla River below and views of Hope Mountain across the valley. After about a half hour's walking, you will come to the Hope–Nicola Valley trailhead, with an information board, a few metres before a yellow gate.

Do not be dismayed by the steep beginning to the Hope-Nicola Trail—the gradient soon eases. As you climb more gently through mixed forest of maples and conifers, or rest at one of the viewpoints, it is not difficult to imagine the trains of laden mules plodding along this same path more than 100 years ago.

About 45 minutes from the trailhead, you will reach the pass—not a spectacular vantage point but a level place between two hills—where a plaque on a tree commemorates the Royal Engineers' mule road to the Similkameen Valley, built in 1860. From here, red metal markers guide your descent to the valley. Follow Hope-Nicola Trail signs to work your way around a gravel pit, prior to stepping out onto Tunnels Road not far from the Coquihalla Canyon Recreation Area parking lot and the next stage in your journey—the Othello-Quintette Tunnels.

B.C. Parks provides a wealth of information about the historic Kettle Valley Railway and its indomitable engineer, Andrew McCulloch. Walking through the tunnels, one can only marvel at the courage and persistence of the men who blasted and built their railway through the 90-m (300-foot) gorge.

Continuing along the railway bed from the final tunnel, you will arrive in a few minutes at the yellow park gate with the familiar Hope-Nicola trailhead just beyond. An easy half-hour walk returns you to your car at Kettle Valley Road.

HEATHER TRAIL

Round trip (to Buckhorn Camp)
10 km (6 miles)
High point 2000 m (6500 feet)
Elevation loss 180 m (600 feet)
Allow 3½ hours

Best July to September
Campgrounds at Cold Spring or
Lightning Lakes in Manning Park
FAMILY HIKE
EASY

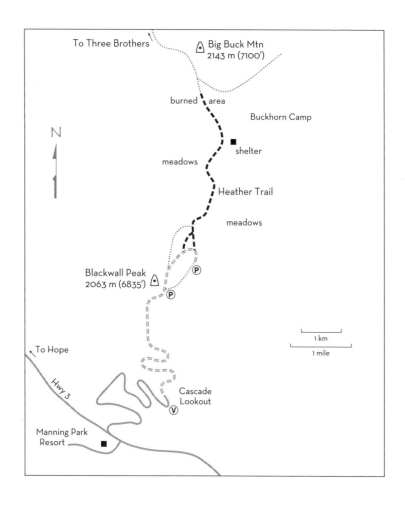

Pink mountain heather

THE OPEN, ROLLING plateau northeast of Allison Pass in Manning Park may be unsuspected by most travellers following the Skagit and Similkameen River valleys between Hope and Princeton. In this high backcountry, miles of subalpine meadows bloom in profusion from mid-July to mid-August. As the snow recedes in late June, first appear the yellow glacier lilies and creamy western anemones, followed by dazzling fields of lupines, paintbrush, valerian, columbine and hellebore. Hugging the earth are mats of tiny saxifrages, phlox and moss campion, while hardy red mountain heather blooms beside the trail.

> GETTING THERE To reach this midsummer idyll, drive east from Hope, via Highways 5 and then 3, for approximately 67 km (42 miles) to Manning Park Lodge. The 15-km (9½-mile) access road to the meadows leaves the north side of Highway 3 almost opposite the lodge, signposted to Cascade Lookout. Stop at the viewpoint and note the mountains identified on the chart—they will be the backdrop to your meadow walk. A good gravel road continues from the lookout to the parking area at the base of Blackwall Peak. Heather Trail can be reached from the lower or upper parking lots.

> THE TRAIL As a family outing, the easy 5 km (3 miles) to the shelter at Buckhorn Camp may be as much as you want to do, though the trail carries on to the first summit of Three Brothers Mountain, often called the First Brother, at 11 km (7 miles) and beyond, for backpackers, to Kicking Horse Camp and Nicomen Lake. As far as Buckhorn Camp, Heather Trail winds mostly downhill through lush vegetation and stands of low-growing alpine fir. There are intermittent views of Frosty Mountain and the Hozameen Range, while ahead of you, sections of the trail can be glimpsed rising through an old burned area toward Big Buck Mountain and the Three Brothers.

For those with energy for a further 2 km (1¼ miles) of climbing, Big Buck is a worthwhile destination, offering 360-degree views and a nodding acquaintance with the First Brother.

Wherever you choose to turn around, the return journey is enhanced by views of mountain ranges to the south and east and by the communication tower atop Blackwall Peak growing ever larger as you approach your starting point.

> **READING LIST**

Baron, Nancy, and John Acorn. *Birds of Coastal British Columbia.*
    Edmonton: Lone Pine Publishing, 1997.
Cannings, Richard, and Sydney Cannings. *British Columbia:*
    A Natural History. 2nd ed. Vancouver: Greystone Books, 2004.
Cousins, Jean. *Nature Walks around Vancouver.* Vancouver:
    Greystone Books, 1997.
Kahn, Charles. *Hiking the Gulf Islands of British Columbia.* 2nd ed.
    Madeira Park, B.C.: Harbour Publishing, 2011.
Murray, Anne. *A Nature Guide to Boundary Bay.* Delta, B.C:
    Nature Guides B.C., 2006.
Nature Vancouver (VNHS). *Parks and Nature Places around*
    Vancouver. Alison Parkinson, ed. Madeira Park, B.C.: Harbour
    Publishing, 2009.
Pojar, Jim, and Andy MacKinnon, eds. *Plants of Coastal British*
    Columbia. 2nd ed. Vancouver: Lone Pine Publishing, 2005.
Stoltmann, Randy. *Hiking Guide to the Big Trees of Southwestern*
    British Columbia. 2nd ed. Vancouver: Western Canada Wilder-
    ness Committee, 1991.

> ALPHABETICAL INDEX OF HIKES

**INDEX OF HIKES BY
LEVEL OF DIFFICULTY**